The Cowboy and the Senorita

A Biography of Roy Rogers and Dale Evans

Howard Kazanjian
and Chris Enss

With a Foreword by Roy "Dusty" Rogers

TWODOT

GUILFORD, CONNECTICUT
HELENA, MONTANA
AN IMPRINT OF THE GLOBE PEQUOT PRESS

A · TWODOT® · BOOK

Copyright © 2005 by Chris Enss and Howard Kazanjian

TwoDot is a registered trademark of Morris Book Publishing, LLC.

Text design by Bill Brown.
All artwork courtesy of the Roy Rogers–Dale Evans family and museum.

Library of Congress Cataloging-in-Publication Data
Kazanjian, Howard.
    The cowboy and the senorita : a biography of Roy Rogers and Dale
 Evans / Howard Kazanjian and Chris Enss ; with a foreword by Roy
 "Dusty" Rogers.— 1st ed.
      p. cm.
    "Roy Rogers filmography": p.
    "Dale Evans filmography": p.
    Includes bibliographical references and index.
    ISBN 978-0-7627-3830-4
    1. Rogers, Roy, 1911– 2. Rogers, Dale Evans. 3. Actors—United
 States—Biography. 4. Singers—United States—Biography. I. Enss,
 Chris, 1961– II. Title.

PN2287.R73K39 2005
791.4302'8'092273—dc22
[B]   2004060612

Manufactured in the United States of America
First Edition/Tenth Printing

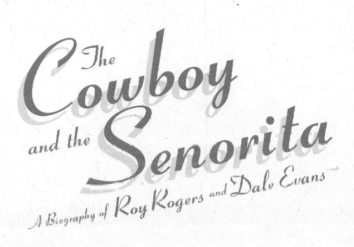

The Cowboy and the Senorita

A Biography of Roy Rogers and Dale Evans

"*The Cowboy and the Senorita*, aptly named after the
first feature film Dale Evans and Roy Rogers acted
in together, is a bittersweet and engrossing book
about the famous couple's amazing ride through life."

—*True West*

"Their real-life story is one the reader will recall long
after the book's cover is closed."

—*ForeWord*

Contents

Foreword vii

Introduction ix

Prologue xii

CHAPTER ONE: Humble Beginnings 1

CHAPTER TWO: Off to California 15

CHAPTER THREE: A Rough Start 25

CHAPTER FOUR: The Pioneer Trio 35

CHAPTER FIVE: Chicago to Hollywood 47

CHAPTER SIX: The Rise of a King 59

CHAPTER SEVEN: Partners on the Celluloid Plains 71

CHAPTER EIGHT: Breaking Trail 83

CHAPTER NINE: Cowboy King Marries Queen of the West 95

CHAPTER TEN: A Higher Calling 107

CHAPTER ELEVEN: Sleeping Angel 121

CHAPTER TWELVE: Faith in a Storm 131

CHAPTER THIRTEEN: Adding to the Family 141

CHAPTER FOURTEEN: One More Hard Trail 155

CHAPTER FIFTEEN: Soldier Son 167

CHAPTER SIXTEEN: Rider in the Sky 179

CHAPTER SEVENTEEN: Long Live the Queen 187

CHAPTER EIGHTEEN: Golden Cloud 195

CHAPTER NINETEEN: The Legend Lives On 201

Epilogue 209

Appendix A: Roy Rogers Filmography 213

Appendix B: Dale Evans Filmography 221

Bibliography 225

Index 231

About the Authors 239

Foreword

It's been said that Roy Rogers and Dale Evans had a more positive influence on the youth of America during the 1930s, '40s, and '50s than any other famous couple in the country. They were heroes to millions of boys and girls—heroes to my brothers and sisters and me as well, but mostly just Mom and Dad.

Over the last sixty years there has been a lot written about my parents and the impact they had on children of all ages. I consider it a testament to their generosity and talent. They remain such beloved western icons that people desire to know more about their lives and, more importantly, the source of their strength in times of great sorrow.

The pages in this new book tell the story of my parents' lives and times in such a way you'll feel you were with them—experiencing their struggles and successes firsthand. Many of the photos have rarely been seen before and will take you back in time. The quotes from fans and celebrities who admired my folks are insightful and endearing and make me very proud. My parents were

Dale Evans and Roy Rogers (opposite page).

Roy and Dusty

ordinary people who lived extraordinary lives. They provided a lifetime of inspiration for myself and millions of moviegoers. Their legend continues.

Thousands of fans visit the Roy Rogers–Dale Evans Museum every year, hoping to relive a simpler time when honest and fair-minded films ruled Saturday matinees and the good guys were good guys both on and off the screen.

—Roy "Dusty" Rogers

Introduction

A stunning young woman in a long, white gown strolled out onto a balcony to take in the full moon of a clear, California sky. Soft music drifted out of the spacious hacienda behind her and mixed with the light breeze that stirred her brown mane. A handsome cowboy followed after the striking lady, singing to her about the night, the stars, and love. She joined him in song, every verse echoing her sentiments about the romantic celluloid moment they found themselves in.

It was a sweet introduction for the two musical actors. Portraying a bashful, but courageous, cowhand and an independent damsel in distress, Roy Rogers and Dale Evans lit up the screen in the Republic feature *The Cowboy and the Senorita*. It was the first film the two appeared in together, one that marked the start of a fifty-six year partnership, both professionally and personally.

Roy and Dale made twenty-nine more movies together, produced and starred in a ten-year hit television series, raised nine children, and enjoyed fifty-two years of marital bliss.

The Cowboy and the Senorita, released in 1944, made their names and lives inseparable.

Cowboy and the Senorita
BIG HIT FOR REPUBLIC

Intrigue and song fill the Old West when America's favorite singing cowboy rides to the rescue of two unfortunate ladies about to be swindled out of their inheritance.

In Republic Pictures' latest film "The Cowboy and the Senorita," Roy Rogers and his sidekick Guinn "Big Boy" Williams, amble into a busy frontier berg looking for work and are mistakenly identified as felons. Roy and Williams' character "Teddy Bear" are accused of kidnapping 17-year-old Chip Martinez, played by Republic Pictures singing sensation, Mary Lee. In truth, Chip has run away from home and her cousin, Ysobel, played by talented newcomer Dale Evans, to hunt for a buried treasure.

Roy convinces Ysobel that he had nothing to do with her cousin's disappearance and offers to help find the teenager. Rearing on his famous palomino Trigger, Roy and Teddy Bear comb the countryside until they find Chip. The pair are then hired on to work at the Martinez ranch and to watch over the impetuous Chip. Desperate to get away again, Chip tells the boys she wants to find the treasure buried in a supposedly worthless gold mine she inherited from her father. They agree to lend the young girl a hand in spite of her cousin's objections.

Meanwhile, Ysobel has promised to sell the mine to her boyfriend Craig Allen, played by John Hubbard. Allen is a charming gambler and town boss who has convinced the unsuspecting Ysobel the mine has no value. Allen of course knows differently.

Using a clue left by Chip's father, Roy investigates the mine and discovers a hidden shaft that contains the gold. The boys must outride Allen's men who are determined to stop Rogers and his sidekick at any cost. Our heroes are in a race against time and a posse. They must get ore samples back to town before the ownership of the mine is transferred.

The action in "The Cowboy and the Senorita" is heightened with several song and dance numbers performed by Roy Rogers, the Sons of the Pioneers, and Dale Evans. Songs include the title tune, "Round Her Neck She Wore A Yellow Ribbon," "Bunk House Bugle Boy," and "Enchilada Man." The chemistry between Roy Rogers and Dale Evans is enchanting and "Big Boy" Williams adds great comic relief as Roy's riding partner.

The King of Cowboys and Trigger will ride the range again this fall in their next picture "The Yellow Rose of Texas." Roy will be paired with Dale Evans for a second time in this feature. He'll be playing an insurance investigator working undercover on Dale's showboat. No doubt Rogers' 900,000 fans will flock to the theatre to watch him ride to the rescue.

Movie Line Magazine, April 1944

Prologue

*Roy Rogers and Dale Evans are every bit the heroes
America and the movies made of them.
To me, they stand as the example of the best things
to come out of Hollywood.*
CLINT BLACK,
country-western singer-songwriter

 hot sun hovered over
more than 8,000 people crowded into the Texas A&M stadium in
College Station. Shoulder to shoulder they sat eagerly awaiting
the arrival of the King of Cowboys and the Queen of the West. A
tidal wave of cheers filled the air as Roy Rogers and Dale Evans
trotted their famous rides into the center of the arena. Over their
long career in film and television, the two had come to represent
truth, justice, and the American way. They were rare celebrities—
adored by fans of every age and walk of life.

The excited onlookers jumped to their feet, applauding and
shouting. Roy reared back on his horse, Trigger Jr., and waved his

Stetson hat at the appreciative audience. Dale blinked away the tears that had welled up in her eyes. It was 1979; more than thirty years had passed since they'd first ridden the range in a series of B-rated westerns.

Since 1938 cowboy lovers had flocked to the theaters to see their pictures, in the process making them the number one box-office draw for twelve years, from 1943 to 1955. Now in their late sixties, the couple had not lost their popularity. They relished the praise of the fans who remembered the time when they ruled the silver-screen West.

The two senior citizens, dressed in matching red, white, and blue spangled western outfits, led their horses to the front of the stands and walked them along the railing. The applause was sustained, and the pair were bombarded with enthusiastic shouts of "We love you, Roy and Dale!" Children stretched their arms out in the hope of shaking hands with the singing cowboy or touching his palomino.

Roy Rogers looked healthy and trim. He sat in his saddle as if he were born there, flashing his familiar smile and squinting eyes over the grateful faces as he strode by. Dale beamed proudly, the lights dancing off her beautiful alabaster skin and cotton-candy gray hair. The cheers from the crowd subsided briefly as Roy and Dale's theme song spilled out of the loudspeakers placed overhead.

Almost as though it had been rehearsed, the massive amateur chorus of onlookers broke into song. "Happy trails to you . . ." Tears streamed down Roy's and Dale's faces. They tried to join in singing, but both were so moved by the outpouring of affection they couldn't utter a note.

Leonard Franklin Slye

Frances Octavia Smith

CHAPTER ONE

Humble Beginnings

*It's hard to imagine there had been another
life, when a boy called Leonard and a girl called
Frances were children; playing, running . . . with no
thought of becoming heroes to millions of kids who
loved Westerns.*

CLARK GABLE, actor

barefoot rider
spurs his midnight-black mare down a dirt road. The horse kicks
up a trail of dust. Its hoofprints leave an imprint on the rolling hill-
side. A strong breeze blows across the soil and begins the work of
erasing them.

The seventeen-year-old horseman, Leonard Slye, is focused on
a distant farmhouse ahead. A whirlwind of dried brush and dirt
encircles the building. Thunder rumbles overhead. Dust is caked in
the lines of Leonard's handsome face, around his squinty, blue
eyes; it powders his clothing. He handles the mare effortlessly.
Rider and horse have come a long way.

Leonard hops off the horse before he pulls it to a stop in front of the white, two-story home. His face holds a worried expression. He races up the stairs leading into the house and throws the door open wide. He skips several steps as he bolts up the rustic staircase to the second floor. From the narrow hallway he can see his father, Andy, lying on a bed. His mother, Mattie, stands over the ailing gentleman, mopping his sweaty brow with a damp cloth. Leonard eases his way toward the room. His strong legs buckle slightly under the weight of overwhelming concern for his father.

Andy's chiseled features are sunken into his head a bit, and his skin is pale. His appearance is a far cry from the robust, energetic man Leonard remembers growing up with. Almost as if he senses his son nearby, Andy turns his tired face toward him and smiles. He weakly waves the teenager into the room. Leonard wastes no time getting to his side. "Did you let them know at the factory I wouldn't be in today?" Andy asks. Leonard nods.

Mattie places a hand on her son's shoulder and gives him a reassuring pat. "He's going to be all right," she says confidently. Leonard looks up at his mother, his worried expression lingering.

Mattie turns and hobbles over to a washbasin on the far side of the room, the hinges on the leg brace she wears creaking slightly as she walks. Polio crippled her when she was a child, but it never slowed her down. Leonard always admired her for that.

He watches Mattie tend to Andy, moved by the devotion and love she has for his father. "Go on now," she coaxes her son. "This farm won't run itself." Leonard does as she asks, glancing back at the pair as he leaves the room. The couple smile warmly at one another. It's a picture of his parents Leonard will hold in his heart forever.

Leonard (left) with his first horse, Babe.

$\mathcal{L}$eonard was the third of four children born to Andrew E. Slye and Mattie Womack Slye, and the only boy. Born on November 5, 1911, in Cincinnati, Ohio, his early years were happy ones, filled with adventure, hard work, and love. His sisters doted on him, and his parents encouraged him in all his endeavors.

Leonard had a remarkable way with animals. He trained his pet skunk, groundhogs, and his horse to perform amazing tricks. He raised chickens and pigs, entering his prize livestock in various farm shows and receiving championship ribbons for his efforts.

He had a particular soft spot for hurt or injured animals. He would mend their broken bones and nurse them back to health. His desire to heal extended beyond four-legged creatures. From the age of eight, he aspired to be a doctor. It was a dream he initially shared only with his mother.

Leonard inherited his ability to dream big from his father. Andy dreamed of escaping the mundane routine of working at the United States Shoe Company where he had been employed for a number of years. He saw himself as an adventurer, a modern-day Robinson Crusoe. He dreamed of exploring the world with his family. When Leonard was still a baby, Andy and his brother built a houseboat and traveled down the Ohio River. The Slye family lived on their floating home for eight years. Eventually, however, Andy realized that his children needed more room to run and play than the deck of the barge had to offer. He decided to dock the boat in Portsmouth, Ohio, and then set his sights on a owning a farm.

Andy returned to the shoe factory in order to earn the money needed to buy a homestead. In 1919 Andy bought a ten-acre farm 12 miles outside Portsmouth, near the country town of Duck Run.

Because Andy knew no other trade than shoemaking, purchasing a farm was a gamble. He and Mattie decided he should keep his job at the factory until the farm could make money. He spent the week in town, returning home on the weekends. In his absence, Leonard, his mother, and his sisters would run the place.

Leonard worked hard and assumed the responsibility of being the man around the house while his father was away. "At the age of seven I had to learn farming, and experience is the best teacher," Leonard would later recall. "We had an old mule and I learned to plow with him. I was so little I had to reach up, to get a hold of the plow handles."

Andy came home on the weekends and helped his wife and children gather eggs, muck out the stalls, and tend to the livestock. The family would relax in the evenings around a potbellied stove and entertain one another singing songs and playing musical instruments. Leonard's parents played the mandolin and the guitar and taught their children to play as well. Leonard was a quick study. He had an exceptional voice and mastered the instruments with ease, going on to learn the clarinet.

Caring for the family farm and keeping up with his schoolwork proved to be overwhelming. In Leonard's junior year of high school, he abandoned the notion of being a doctor, dropped out, and went to work at the shoe factory with his father. Mattie was troubled by his decision and urged him to reconsider. "I don't want you wasting away in a factory," she told him. "It makes a man tired and sick in his spirit. It's a prison sentence to men with big dreams." Leonard knew only too well what she meant. He had watched his father's pioneer spirit dwindle from a flame to a flicker holed up inside a noisy workshop cutting leather for shoe soles. Andy longed to be outside on his farm. Leonard was no different. But his desire to earn a living overshadowed his fondness for the great outdoors.

In an effort to satisfy his mother's wishes for him to earn his high school diploma, he enrolled in night school. He wore himself out trying to keep up with the job at the factory, maintaining the farm, and studying. He fell asleep in class one evening and was so embarrassed by the experience he gave up night school altogether.

Leonard was then able to spend more time at home with his father, and his heart broke for the man. He felt Andy's failing health could be attributed to the monotony of his factory chores. One night Leonard stole into his father's room to talk to him about an idea he'd been mulling over. He was convinced there was a better way of earning a living and had considered quitting his job in favor of playing guitar for square dances. Maybe even moving out of the area to pursue his dream.

Leonard sat next to his father and smiled down at him lying in bed. "Pop," he began. "I've saved up ninety-one bucks, and you ought to have about a hundred, I reckon. What d'you say we quit the factory and drive out to California to visit Mary?" Mary was Leonard's sister; she lived in Lawndale with her husband. "She's said it's fine country," Leonard added. "We could probably get jobs out there."

Andy raised himself up on his elbows and smiled a smile as big as the horizon. The mere notion of such a trip worked as an elixir for his soul. Mattie looked in on the two, now chattering away about the possibilities that lay ahead for the Slye family.

Within a month Leonard, his parents, and two of his sisters were traveling the narrow concrete highways toward California.

The woman who would become a key figure in his life and career was not far behind. She would be heading west from a small town in the Texas panhandle.

*L*ights from a giant marquee over a dilapidated movie house in Gretna Green, Texas, pierced through the dark street stretched out before the building. Black letters over the bright, white sign read, RIDERS OF THE PURPLE SAGE STARRING TOM MIX AND WHERE THE WORST BEGINS STARRING RUTH ROLAND.

An anxious group of nine- and ten-year-old boys and girls raced up to the box office and exchanged their nickels for a ticket. Clutching their prize, they hurried into the theater. From the lobby they could hear that the cartoon had already started. A cranky usher dressed in red, military-style garb tore the children's tickets and pointed them in the direction of the screening. Hurrying past the refreshment stand, they nearly ran headlong into a teenage girl named Frances Fox, standing just outside a phone booth.

Frances was an attractive young lady with dark features and a slim figure. She was so preoccupied she barely took notice of the excited children as they burst through the theater doors.

She reluctantly stepped inside the phone booth. She sighed a long, heavy sigh and blinked away a tear as she picked up the receiver and deposited coins into the machine. Frances timidly asked the operator to connect her to the Smith residence in Uvalde, Texas. It rang twice before anyone on the other end picked it up.

The frail voice of an older woman answered. Frances said nothing for a moment. She was too nervous to speak. "Mother?" she finally asked.

"Oh, thank God. Frances is it you? Are you all right?" came the response.

Frances assured her mother that she was well. Her mother confirmed what the teenager already knew: Her parents had been worried about her. It was Monday, and their fourteen-year-old daughter had been gone all weekend.

"I have good news," Frances blurted out. "I'm married." An awful, throbbing silence passed between them. Walter and Betty Sue Smith were shocked at their first child's admission.

When they'd last spoken with Frances, she had told them she was going to a play rehearsal at school and then spending the night with a girlfriend. Now their only daughter had eloped. Frances went on to tell them that she and the boy she had been secretly seeing had driven across the state line into Tennessee and tied the knot.

"We want you to come home," Betty Sue softly urged. "We'll work this out and you can go back to school." Frances was a junior in high school with exceptional grades. "You can graduate in another year."

Frances said no. "All I want now is to be a good wife and to start a home of my own," she explained. Another wave of silence fell over the mother and daughter.

Betty Sue had been afraid this would happen. She'd thought Frances was too young to date at thirteen, but she'd agreed to let her attend courthouse dances while acting as her daughter's chaperone. It was at one of those dances that Frances met her first steady, a boy in his late teens who was now her husband. Walter and Betty Sue had realized the two were spending too much time together and forbade Frances from seeing him, but the pair were determined to be together.

Frances at fourteen years old (opposite page).

Frances's early rebellion was not driven by an unhappy home life. "I had a wonderful childhood," she would later recall. "I never lacked attention and I loved that." Instead she attributed her impetuous actions to being young and madly in love.

Frances Octavia Smith was born on October 31, 1912. Her father was a farmer and the owner-operator of a hardware store. Her mother was a homemaker. Walter and Betty Sue were musically inclined. Walter sang gospel songs, and Betty Sue played the piano. They nurtured their two children's love for music. Frances and her brother, Hillman, had fine singing voices. Frances made her singing debut at the family church at the age of three. It was then that she began dreaming of being a performer. In addition to being talented, she was very bright. In a short time Frances had skipped several grades in school. By the time she was twelve, she was a freshman in high school.

Walter and Betty Sue believed their children were capable of great things. They were disappointed that Frances had sidelined her creative aspirations to get married.

Betty Sue said of her daughter, "Frances is too impulsive; she means well, but she rushes into things before she thinks them through."

Frances and her new husband, Thomas Fox, moved in with his parents in Blytheville, Arkansas. He went to work for his father, but the pair had a difficult time settling into domestic life. Tom was restless and left her twice in their first six months of marriage. She was miserable and pregnant when Walter and Betty Sue relocated to Memphis and invited Frances to move in with them.

Frances and her brother, Hillman, on a mule at their grandfather's ranch in Texas.

She agreed, hoping her husband would follow after her and their unborn child. When their son, Tom Jr., was born, he was by her side. But he would soon leave again, and this time for good. Days after his abrupt departure, he sent a letter to Frances telling her their marriage had been a mistake and that he was too young to be tied down to a wife and son. He wanted a divorce. No amount of pleading from Frances would change his mind.

Frances's parents offered to help her raise her baby and to help her get back on her feet. Heartbroken and feeling very much alone, she agreed, but strongly objected to her parents' suggestion that they adopt her son. "He was the shining light of my life," she would say. "Tommy Fox was my child, I loved him dearly, and it would be I who would take care of him."

It wasn't until a year after her son was born that she could bring herself to file for divorce. At seventeen she was a single mother in search of a way to provide for her boy. Her stellar grades enabled her to enroll in business school without a high school diploma. But while a job in the corporate world would put food on the table, her ultimate career goal leaned more toward the creative. She wanted to sing and write music. Until such an opportunity arose, she provided for herself and her son as a secretary at an insurance company— a secretary who wrote music in her spare time.

Frances sits alone at her desk at work. It's lunchtime, and everyone is out of the office. A blank accident claim form is waiting in the typewriter for her to fill out. She sits with her fingers poised over the keys, humming.

Her eyes shift from the form to a picture of her baby on the corner of the desk. She hums louder as she glances out the window at the mountains in the near distance, then breaks into a chorus of a song no one but her has heard before. She snatches up a nearby piece of paper and jots down the lyrics. She reads over the tune and begins singing what she's written.

"There's a ceiling of blue above, and some trees peaceful as a dove. No wonder that people love hazy mountains . . ."

She smiles to herself. For a moment she sees beyond her hardships and is at center stage, singing for an audience, her parents, and her little boy.

Leonard, his mother, and his father on their way to California.

CHAPTER TWO

Off to California

As a kid, I was Roy Rogers, and my neighbor was
Hopalong Cassidy. We fought the wars of Altadena.
STEVE SCHOENBAUM, *53, Roy Rogers fan*
as quoted in the Los Angeles Times,
May 5, 2003

full moon lit up the
desert sky over Southern California, spilling out onto a rustic
migrant workers' camp below. Leonard Slye, his face sunburned
and chapped, glanced up at the numerous stars as he turned the
skinned rabbit skewered on a stick he was holding over a fire. His
mother, Mattie, and sisters Cleda and Kathleen sat around a
weather-beaten tent, dishing meager servings of beans and wheat
cakes onto plates. Leonard's father, Andy, had parked himself next
to him, poring over a tattered map.

"Our luck is sure to change out here, Len," he said to his son.
Leonard smiled and nodded. The aroma from the cooked meat
wafted through the air, and he licked his lips. The Slye family
would be eating good tonight.

It was the spring of 1930, and Andy Slye and his clan were among thousands who had departed the Midwest. Many were escaping the devastating conditions of the Dust Bowl.

Drought and hard times had robbed them of their homes and possessions, driving them to California with great hopes for their future. Even in California, however, jobs were scarce, and discouraged farm families were forced to take jobs picking fruit.

Disaster did not drive the Slyes west, but they were lured to the coast for the same reasons as everyone else—a better life. Leonard and his father had depleted their funds getting the family to this point and needed money to get them back on their feet. They, too, were forced to take work picking grapes and peaches.

The work was hard, but steady. They'd not been able to afford much in the way of food; the rabbit Leonard was cooking represented the only meat his family had had to eat in he didn't know how long. He'd hunted the animal down with his slingshot.

From behind the trees and brush, Leonard caught a glimpse of some of the children who lived at the camp. They were staring intently at the fire and appeared hypnotized by the aroma of fried rabbit. Leonard watched the sad-faced, weary boys and girls inch their way over to him. He knew what they were thinking.

He glanced over at his mother, who nodded approvingly, then cut the rabbit up into as many portions as possible. The children quickly devoured the feast.

After the Slye family finished their beans and cakes, they removed their guitar and mandolin from their rickety, 1923 Dodge truck and began to play. The children clapped and danced around. Their parents wandered over, joining in the music with instruments like harmonicas and juice harps. A makeshift dance floor was quickly put together using scraps of lumber, and the camp followers square danced to Leonard's calls.

Leonard was moved by the sheer abandon the disenfranchised families were experiencing. In the midst of their trials, they let themselves be swept away with the song. They came alive. The music did something to the spirit of the hungry, depressed people, and Leonard liked being a part of it. He felt as if was helping people—something he'd wanted to do as a boy when he dreamed of being a doctor.

A tall unassuming man, not much older than Leonard, carrying a writing pad and circling the dance floor, caught his eye. He wore a serious expression and seemed to be drinking in the atmosphere, then capturing the moment with pen and paper. The man would later describe a scene similar to this in the novel *The Grapes of Wrath.*

The laborers and their families allowed themselves a few hours of fun, then departed to their tents to bed down for the night. What Leonard remembered most about migrant camp life was that although material goods were in short supply, there was plenty of happiness and music.

It had been a two-week drive from Ohio to California. The Slye truck, loaded down with suitcases, tents, canned goods and guitars, faithfully transported the family to their destination, breaking down only twice along the way. They traveled via Route 66—a bumpy, two-lane highway empty of hotels or rest stops. Much like the pioneers of the 1800s, the Slyes encountered hostile weather and rough terrain on their way to the Golden State. The minor setbacks never deterred them from their goal. California would afford Leonard opportunities he never imagined.

This was Leonard's second trip west with his family. The first time they'd come to California, they had stayed with his sister Mary and her husband in Lawndale. The Slyes loved the warm climate and wide-open spaces California had to offer.

Leonard and his father quickly got work driving trucks for a road construction company, but after four months Andy decided it best they head back to the farm in Duck Run. Not long after they returned to Ohio, they began missing the West Coast. Leonard ached to see the broad blue sky and feel the sunshine on his back. When Mary's father-in-law decided to leave Duck Run and move out to California, Leonard went with him. Not long after that, Andy and Mattie sold their Ohio homestead and set off for the West Coast again. This time, jobs weren't as easy to come by.

Picking fruit was welcome work, but it was grueling and paid very little. In the fall the work tapered off altogether. Andy and Leonard needed steady employment. Andy heard about a shoe factory in Los Angeles that was hiring and approached his son about the prospect.

The resignation in his eyes shook Leonard to his core. Andy wore the dread of being cooped up in a factory in every line on his face. "A man takes what's available to him," he told Leonard. "You coming along?" A long silence passed between the two. Leonard wanted to talk him out of it, but what other options had he to offer? "No, Pop," he finally said. "No factory for me." Andy studied his son's face for a moment, waiting for him to volunteer his plans.

"The only thing I have an honest good feeling for is music," Leonard confessed. "It makes me happy, and my playing and singing seems to make everyone else happy. I'd like to take a try at being a musician," he concluded.

Andy admired the dreamer and understood more than anyone could at that moment just what Leonard was telling him.

"I'd be crazy to say that I know how it will work out," Leonard added. "But I'll never know until I try."

"A man should do something he enjoys doing," Andy told him. "I've always felt like a slave making shoes. Probably you're right." He wished his boy well and headed off for the shoe factory alone.

Leonard talked his mandolin-playing cousin, Stanley Slye, into joining him and forming a duo. He sold him on the idea that they could earn a living playing for social meetings, parties, and square dances. "Some of the better groups are working on the radio a lot," Leonard added confidently. And so the Slye Brothers was born. The boys managed to play for a few events in the area, but not for pay. The only money they made was when they passed the hat and partygoers made contributions.

One particular evening the Slye Brothers got a boost to their bruised egos when a swarthy man approached them at the conclusion of their show. He told the pair that he was an agent and wanted to represent them. For a brief moment Leonard and Stanley thought they were on their way to the big time. Their new agent arranged a couple of jobs for the duo, but no money was ever forthcoming. He explained to the brothers that the funds they earned were somehow eaten up by expenses. The agent disappeared not long after that, and the boys went back to business as usual—a little wiser than before.

The Slye Brothers continued to play for a few events here and there, but they still weren't making much money and Stanley was getting discouraged. He summonded Leonard to a meeting to discuss their career. "We're getting nowhere fast," Stanley told his partner. "I'm ready to call it quits and see if I can find a job that has a paycheck." Leonard understood his concern. He'd entertained those same thoughts from time to time. It was decided that the Slye Brothers' career should come to an end. Stanley went off

*Leonard (left) at one of his many "one-night-only" performances
early in his career.*

to find a nine-to-five position, and Leonard was left to ponder his
musical fate. After careful consideration he realized he wasn't
ready to abandon his dream.

Leonard signed on with a musical group known as Uncle Tom Murray's Hollywood Hillbillies. Uncle Tom never offered Leonard a salary for his contribution. He convinced the younger man that experience was more valuable than money. Leonard again had to take stock of his situation and make a decision. Should he continue with the Hollywood Hillbillies or go it alone? He turned to a family member who had always been a strong supporter.

Leonard's sister Mary sang with him at family get-togethers. They harmonized beautifully, and she believed he had talent. Although he was quite bashful, she pushed him to sing solos for people other than their relatives. "He's a charming boy with a good voice," Mary told her parents. "Given half a chance I think he can do wonders." Mattie and Andy agreed.

Leonard's opportunity to "do wonders" finally came by way of a small radio station in Inglewood. Station KMCS was hosting an amateur singing contest on a program called *The Midnight Frolic*. Mary and Mattie urged Leonard to enter. It took a bit of talking to persuade him that it could be the break he was looking for. "I don't mind calling square dances, or singing among a few friends," Leonard told them. "But I'm not sure about singing in front of strangers." When he finally agreed, everyone in the family was excited and pledged to do all they could to help him get ready.

While Leonard practiced for the event, his mother and sister worked on putting together a proper western outfit for his debut. Mary stitched a patchwork of bright-colored squares onto one of his old shirts, and Mattie pressed his lone pair of cowboy trousers. When the big day finally arrived, Leonard scooped up his twenty-dollar guitar and, with his family in tow, set out for the radio station.

The studio audience was jammed with people wanting to participate in the contest. The Slyes arrived just before midnight and took their seats among the hopeful singers and musicians. Leonard

Left to right: Mary, Kathleen, Mrs. Slye, Leonard, Mr. Slye, and Cleda.

was nervous. Looking around the room, he studied the faces of the people he was thoroughly convinced were far better than he was. By three o'clock in the morning, *The Midnight Frolic* amateur contest was still going strong. Leonard would be next up to the microphone. When the show's master of ceremonies introduced him, he didn't make a move. He was paralyzed with fear and clutched the neck of his guitar as if it had frozen in his hand.

Mary elbowed her brother a couple of times. When he didn't move, she poked him hard in the ribs. Then she got up from her seat, bent down in front of him, and looked him straight in the eyes. "Len," she said firmly. "We've come all the way down here to hear you sing. I sewed that fancy shirt for you and Mama ironed your pants. Now get up there!" Leonard still didn't move. Mary grabbed his arm and pulled him to his feet. "You get up there and show them how good you can play and sing," she concluded.

Leonard made his way to the stage and, after an awkward moment or two, began strumming his guitar and singing. He played a couple of old hillbilly tunes, the ones he'd grown up singing. He watched his folks clapping along with the music, and that eased his nervousness. At the end of the set, the audience erupted in applause. A broad smile crept across Leonard's scarlet face.

Leonard Slye didn't win the contest. He didn't even place, but before he left the studio the people at the radio station took his name down. The next day he received a call from the manager of a western musical group, The Rocky Mountaineers. He wanted to know if Leonard would be interested in signing up with the band. "We've got a weekly program going on a Long Beach radio station," the manager explained. "And while we don't get any pay for playing, we are given the privilege of plugging our own services over the air. So that means a few pay jobs."

Leonard didn't have to think about the offer long. He jumped at the chance to be a part of a real musical outfit.

An early promotional picture taken when Frances worked for radio station WHAS in Louisville, Kentucky.

CHAPTER THREE

A Rough Start

She was feisty, daring, could hold her own
against any band of bad guys and looked good
enough to leave them dreaming of her at night,
and what a voice. . . .

CYBILL SHEPHERD, *actress*

winter storm blanketed the already saturated Chicago streets with snow. Icy winds blasted through the loose insulation around the windows in Frances Smith's tiny, one-room apartment. She forced a smile at her five-year-old son, Tommy, pulled him to the kitchen table, and served him a meager breakfast. He lapped up every bite happily. Frances pushed her hair off her tired face and choked back a tear. Her skin was pale, making the dark circles under her eyes all the more pronounced. She was tempted to sample her son's meal, but decided against it. She was hungry. It was 1931, and the country was in the midst of a depression; everyone was hungry. Frances was determined her child would not go without food even if it meant she had to give up a meal or two to make that happen.

After a four-year stay in Tennessee, Frances felt a move to Illinois was necessary. She hoped to advance her singing career in Chicago performing on one of the powerful Chicago stations that reached far and deep into the heartland of America. While in Memphis she had managed to go from singing on a thirty-minute request show to hosting a program on the largest station in town. If she could conquer Chicago, she'd have it made.

Music spilled out of a radio in the corner of the room, the tunes occasionally interrupted by newscasts announcing the closure of another bank or stories about desperate stockholders jumping out of windows. It was a trying time for everyone. Frances sought to comfort herself with that truth, but it was no use. Tommy finished his meal and entertained himself with a few of his toys. She watched him play as she dressed for work at the Goodyear Company, where her duties included filing, taking dictation, and answering phones.

Frances made twenty-five dollars a week. More than half of her income went to pay for Tommy's sitter; the other half went to pay for rent and food. Often there was precious little in the way of groceries in the cupboards.

However dismal the world was around her, she pressed on, clinging to the dream that she could change their lives for the better.

Frances seized every opportunity to audition as a performer at various clubs around town but had no luck. Club owners and talent scouts weren't that impressed with her Memphis accomplishments. She'd been in the city for two years and nothing seemed to be working out as she had hoped. As her weak fingers fastened the buttons on Tommy's coat, she pondered how alone they truly were. She held him close to her and reminded him how much she loved him and always would. Tears were standing in her eyes. Tommy knew something was wrong. He studied his mother's face. She looked faint.

Frances and her son Tom in Chicago.

Frances was very ill. Earlier in the week she had been to see a doctor, and the diagnosis was acute malnutrition. She had been warned that if she didn't take care of the condition, she could die. "When do I stop beating my head against this wall, Tommy?" she asked him rhetorically. The thought of getting on the train to go to work exhausted her. "I came out here to crack Chicago," she confessed. "But Chicago has cracked me." She decided right then to wire her parents and ask them for help.

She vowed to herself that once she was well she'd get right back in the game—nothing would deter her for long.

Frances's parents, Walter and Betty Sue, met their daughter and grandson at the train. It had been a long, hard trip back to Italy, Texas, where her mom and dad had relocated a few years prior. Frances looked miserable. Betty Sue scooped Tommy up with one arm and squeezed her daughter's neck with the other. Walter was happy to see them come home as well. Frances was unsteady on her feet, dizzy from hunger. Her mother and father took her straight to the hospital. After a two-week stay she went to her parents' home to continue recuperating.

Three months would pass before she would be on her feet again. She spent that time in bed resting. From the upstairs window of the farmhouse, she watched her son playing with the animals and enjoying the sunshine. As the healthy glow returned to Frances's cheeks, so did her desire to continue her singing career. She set her sights on musical comedies and Broadway. To start, she settled for a job in radio and Louisville, Kentucky.

With Tommy in tow Frances made the move and began work at station WHAS as one of their featured singers. She was well paid to sing popular tunes like "Shine On, Harvest Moon" and "You Are My Sunshine."

She had auditioned for the staff position using the stage name of Marion Lee. The program director disapproved of the stage name and quickly renamed her. "Your name is now Dale Evans," he informed her. Frances was aghast. "That's a boy's name!" she fired back. "And what does Evans have to do with me?" He explained that the name *Dale* was from a silent-movie actress he admired and the name *Evans* just had a nice ring to it. "It will be easy for the announcers to pronounce and impossible to misspell," he concluded. She couldn't argue with that. Frances Smith left the director's office Dale Evans.

Monday through Friday at six thirty in the morning, announcer Joe Pierson would step up to the microphone and introduce Dale and the five-piece band she was singing with. "And now help me welcome Honey and the Flapjacks," he would say. Dale shared the stage with many aspiring entertainers from that time, musicians who regularly played at the Grand Ole Opry. Some days the halls of the station would be flooded with ambitious performers and their instruments, guitars and fiddles as far as the eye could see lining the walls leading into the studio. Surrounded by talent and promise, Dale Evans believed she was finally on her way, but her hardships continued.

At the end of another long, hard workday, Dale hurried home to her son. She sighed as she eyed the stairs leading to their third-floor apartment. She was tired, and they seemed to go on forever. The lady who looked after Tommy stood at the top of the landing waiting for Dale. She looked worried and was wringing her hands.

"What's wrong?" Dale asked. The sitter swallowed her hysteria and told her that Tommy was ill. "He's been vomiting most of the day," she explained. "His arms and legs have been hurting him so bad he just screams with pain." A thought pierced Dale's heart like a dagger. Could Tommy be suffering from polio? Kentucky was experiencing a polio epidemic that had killed or crippled hundreds of children. Dale's face turned white. It can't be, she whispered to herself.

The two women hurried inside the apartment and into Tommy's room. Tears rolled down his cheeks as he rubbed his arms. Dale rushed her son to the hospital. The doctor's agreed with Dale's suspicions and advised that Tommy be tested for polio.

Dale waited outside of the examination room for word about her son's condition. A spinal tap was ordered, and Dale waited for the results in the hospital chapel.

"Lord," she pleaded, "I'll do anything . . . I'll forget about show business. I'll read my Bible every day and I'll pray and be faithful to you. I promise to put you first in my life," she cried. Waiting for the test results was agonizing. When the doctor finally told Dale the news that Tommy did not have polio and would be all right, she sobbed for joy.

With Tommy safely back at home, life returned to normal. Despite her best intentions, however, Dale gradually strayed from the bargain she'd made with God. She was fiercely devoted to her son and her career, but it would take another grave experience for her to see that Tommy was entitled to more attention. Dale's neighbor's daughter had been playing around a pile of burning leaves when the hem of her dress caught fire. The girl's mother arrived home from work just in time to see her engulfed in flames. She tried to save her daughter, but it was too late. The child died en route to the hospital. Dale feared something like that happening to Tommy in her absence. After careful consideration, she decided to relocate her family to the place Tommy had been the happiest.

Walter and Betty Sue again welcomed their daughter and grandson home. Tommy was in his element. He thrived on the wide-open spaces and the extended family that showered him with affection. Feeling much more secure about her son's welfare, Dale set out to look for work. She found employment at WFAA radio in Dallas as the lead singer for a band that performed on *The Early Bird* program.

The Early Bird show featured a variety of acts from orchestras to comedians, and Dale entertained the live studio audience with renditions of popular tunes like "Mockingbird Hill" and "If I Only Had a Nickel." Listeners enjoyed her singing, and in a short time she had created a following. Her regional popularity was given a boost in August 1938 when she appeared on the cover of *Rural Radio Magazine.* Offers for work poured in. She accepted engagements to sing at posh dinner and country clubs and at hotels with full orchestra. And then a gentleman came calling. . . .

Robert Butts was a pianist and orchestral arranger who had become interested in Dale when they met in Louisville. He was making his way to the West Coast via Dallas when he phoned and asked if Dale would see him when he was in town. She happily agreed.

Robert was immensely talented, and Dale mentioned his musical abilities to the manager of WFAA. Not long after his arrival, Robert was hired on as a pianist and arranger for the station.

Dale lived in Dallas during the week and traveled to Italy on the weekends to spend time with Tommy, her brother, and her parents. For a year and a half, Dale managed to make time in Dallas and Italy for outings with Robert. In December 1939 Robert

proposed, and Dale accepted. The two were married and decided to move to Chicago. She was convinced that, given another chance, she could make her mark there, but this time she gave in to her parents' request and left Tommy with them.

Chicago wasn't as cold and unforgiving as Dale remembered it from before. Robert was hired as a composer-arranger for the NBC radio affiliate. Dale joined the Jay Mills Orchestra and sang jazz numbers for guests at the Edgewater Beach Hotel. She was becoming a recognizable voice in the area and was a much-sought-after jazz vocalist for many bands—a fact she found comforting once she realized the Jay Mills Orchestra was the wrong job for her.

Night after night Dale would sit off to one side of the stage watching as the other vocalist with the Jay Mills group serenaded the dignified clientele with beautiful ballads. The audience showered the other vocalist with applause that transcended the polite response Dale received for her jazz numbers. The high-society patrons who frequented the hotel along the lakeshore appreciated the effort but were clearly unsatisfied. So was Dale. When she was offered a chance to audition for Anson Weeks's popular orchestra, she jumped at the chance. Weeks had played for and recorded with some of the most famous singers of the day. Bing and Bob Crosby, Carl Ravazza, and Kay St. Germain were among the many artists who worked with the Weeks orchestra. Dale was offered the job as Anson Weeks's lead vocalist and she immediately accepted. She prayed the move would lead her to Broadway.

A 1938 publicity photo of Dale (opposite page).

Leonard (right) and Farley's Gold Star Rangers.

CHAPTER FOUR

The Pioneer Trio

*With their glorious three-part harmonies
and sophisticated musical arrangements, the
Sons of the Pioneers define the genre known as
Western music. . . .*
WILL ROGERS, *1935*

ragtag group of
seven singers and musicians stared happily into a camera lens
waiting for the picture to snap. They posed with their fiddles, ban-
jos, and guitars in front of an old barn door—a fitting backdrop for
the first and last promotional photograph of the struggling western group the Rocky Mountaineers. It was 1932, and although
band member Leonard Slye's face appeared thin and gaunt in the
picture, it did not detract from the excited gleam in his eyes. He
was living a dream.

Along with Leonard some of the talent among the Rocky Mountaineers were baritone and yodeler Tim Spencer, and singer-songwriter Bob Nolan. These were men who would go on to be giants in the western music industry, but for now they were simply ambitious entertainers in search of a venue to perform.

These were lean years for Leonard and the other band members, who played for square dances and barn raisings for little or no pay—just for the chance to entertain. They depended on the kindness of music lovers and the understanding of Mountaineer wives to keep them fed and provide them with a place to sleep.

The intervals between musical engagements seemed forever for Leonard. There were occasions when he questioned his pursuit, but ultimately he held to the belief that in the end he would be able to make a living singing and strumming his guitar. Nothing could persuade him to lay his ambition aside and return to life working in a factory like his father. He was determined to stay the course.

The Rocky Mountaineers would eventually fold, when hungry members of the band traded in their quest of a record contract for a steady paycheck. Leonard replaced the musicians with other dreamers with names like Cactus Mac, Cyclone, and Slumber Nichols. These men, along with Leonard and Tim, created the western group the International Cowboys. Leonard felt the handle was appropriate because each member of the band had a different ethnic background.

The International Cowboys managed to play their way onto an overnight radio show in Orange County. A booking agent heard the band and called the station the following day. The Cowboys were encouraged by the agent's enthusiasm for their style and sound and quickly jumped at his offer to set them up at an engagement at the Warner Theater in downtown Los Angeles.

The 2,500-seat Warner was a relatively new venue, having opened in 1931. In 1933, after changing the band's name to the O-Bar-O Cowboys (at the request of the agent), Leonard and the other musicians stepped on stage and stared out over the sparsely filled seats. Just as the band began to play, a massive earthquake rocked the theater. The frightened audience leapt up and raced out of the building, leaving the Cowboys alone. They'd never play the Warner again.

The O-Bar-O Cowboys' agent convinced Leonard and the others that they needed to take their act on a tour of the Southwest: Arizona, New Mexico, Texas, places where western music was coming into its own. The musicians agreed and loaded their instruments and belongings into a run down Ford and headed out.

The agent, however, failed to inform the press of the Cowboys' arrival in Miami, Arizona. Consequently, no one attended their first scheduled performance. The next day Leonard's band mates decided to let the town know they were there. They rented a megaphone and announced their upcoming show from their car as they drove around the neighborhoods. The second performance fared only a bit better than the night before—the little money earned was used to gas up the band's vehicle.

Leonard gave up his wristwatch to pay the outstanding debt the Cowboys owed for their stay at a trailer park, and then the band pressed on. Wilcox was the next stop, and from there they headed to New Mexico. Along the way Leonard hunted with a borrowed rifle to provide them all with much of their food. They sustained themselves on meals of jackrabbit and deer meat. When the band arrived in Roswell, they were craving home-cooked dinners that did not include wild game.

Leonard on the road with the O-Bar-O Cowboys.

The local radio station, KRNC, invited the Cowboys into the studio for an interview and to give them a chance to perform. During their talk with the announcer, each of the band members was asked what he missed most from home since he'd been on the road.

Every member mentioned a type of food in the hope the listening audience would take pity on them and offer up the items they mentioned. "I'd just about give my right arm for a piece of lemon pie like Mom makes back home," Leonard confessed. Sure enough a cheerful caller phoned in and offered to bake a pie for him if he would sing the Swiss yodel. Driven by the thought of sinking his teeth into such a tasty dessert, he let out a yodel to end all yodels. The pleased caller promised to deliver the lemon pie as soon as it was out of the oven.

Leonard returned to his hotel room that afternoon confident that before the evening was out he would be eating like a king. He smacked his lips as he watched the road leading up to the inn. Finally, a car pulled into the drive. A pair of women stepped out of the vehicle, each carrying a lemon pie. Leonard hurried out to meet them—but when his eyes fell on the young woman driver, he momentarily forgot about his stomach. Leonard was captivated by the ash-blond beauty with the quiet, gentle manner. Grace Arline Wilkins—who went by Arline—was equally smitten with Leonard. Arline's mother presented the second pie to the other ravenous members of the band, and they breathed in the aroma.

Mrs. Wilkins took pity on the hungry bunch and asked the Cowboys to have dinner at their home. Arline gave Leonard an approving smile as he quickly accepted the invitation. The ladies loaded into their car and drove away. Once the vehicle had disappeared from sight, the boys tore into the pie.

The O-Bar-O Cowboys stayed in Roswell for two weeks, playing for dances and special events. Leonard and Arline spent a lot of time together during the band's New Mexico stop. A Lions Club square dance provided the group with the funds they needed to return to Los Angeles, and as the day of Leonard's departure neared the two promised to continue their friendship by mail. They eagerly looked forward to the time when they would see each other again.

The moderate success the musicians had enjoyed in New Mexico did not follow them back to Los Angeles. In fact, performance dates for the O-Bar-O Cowboys were so few and far between that the group eventually disbanded. Leonard joined another ensemble called Jack and His Texas Outlaws. He kept Arline informed of their activities, or lack thereof, and shared with her his disappointment when that band folded as well.

Despite the alternating success and discouragement that inevitably accompanied building a career in the music business, Leonard Slye would not give up on his aspirations. He decided to give his dreams of being an entertainer one more try. Leonard and Tim Spencer founded yet another group and persuaded Bob Nolan to join them. The men called themselves the Pioneer Trio and quickly landed a regular spot on KFWB. They found a boarding-house within walking distance of the station in Hollywood where they could live for a modest $9.00 a week—three meals included. After settling in, they began writing original songs and practicing the smooth harmonies and wistful western sound that would one day become their trademark.

Journalist Bernie Milligan became a fan of the boys and frequently included the Pioneer Trio in the column he penned for the *Los Angeles Herald Examiner*, called "Best Bets of the Day."

"This group has the finest arrangements!" he wrote in 1934. "They are a good singing trio that perfects mellow, three part harmony yodeling. The yodeling is put together with jazzy fiddle playing and syncopated singing."

The added publicity and positive reviews helped the Pioneer Trio acquire steady work. They opened their shows with a song Billy Hill wrote titled "The Last Roundup."

It soon became one of the most popular tunes around. After years of struggling, Leonard was finally seeing his career take hold. Bookings for the band poured in.

In light of the group's growing popularity, KFWB radio sought to make the Pioneer Trio a permanent fixture at the station. The boys were offered a contract that would pay them $35 a week for two shows a day. It was an impressive amount for the young man from Ohio. Leonard later recalled that "it was like a million dollars" to him.

Announcer Harry Hall opened KFWB's afternoon program one day with a cowboy yell and a hearty welcome to all listeners. The Pioneer Trio waited patiently behind a bank of microphones. After their introductions the group would begin serenading the audience. "Our musical program today is sponsored by the Farley Clothing Company," Harry proudly stated. "And now, here are the Sons of the Pioneers."

Leonard, Bob, and Tim exchanged a confused look. Who were the Sons of the Pioneers?

An awkward silence hung in air for a second or two. Finally Harry nodded to the boys, and they began playing. Off the air the group pointed out the announcer's error. "You're too young to be pioneers," Harry explained. The trio agreed and decided to adopt the new brand.

The Sons of the Pioneers were indeed a Southern California favorite. In 1936 columnist Ray De O'Fan of the *Los Angeles Times* summed up the popular opinion of the band: "Eating, sleeping, driving, working, or playing their haunting melodies seek me out and taunt me."

Eventually news of the band's phenomenal sound spread throughout the state. Leonard Slye and the other members were elated and grateful for the praise and the attention. They were sought after to play at rodeos, nightclub, and fund-raising events. For Leonard the most memorable event the group was asked to perform at was a benefit for the Salvation Army in San Bernardino. The presence of the Sons of the Pioneers at this function came by way of invitation from Will Rogers. The cowboy humorist was a personal hero of Leonard's, and he eagerly looked forward to meeting and playing for the American legend.

Before the Sons of the Pioneers took the stage, the witty Rogers introduced himself to the group. Leonard was impressed with his generosity and down-to-earth manner. After the band finished with the show, Rogers visited the boys backstage, shook their hands, and thanked them for coming. He then left the benefit and headed off to the airport.

From there Rogers was heading to Alaska, where, on August 15, 1935, just a few days after crossing the benefit stage and expressing his appreciation to the audience for participating, he died when his plane went down near Point Barrow. The Sons of the Pioneers were among the last to see the columnist alive. Years later, Leonard and band mate Tim Spencer visited the site of the crash. "He went through hardships and came out with his wit intact," Leonard would say in 1993. "He looked at America from the poor man's side of things, not from the point of view of the rich bankers and powerful politicians who usually get their thoughts heard."

Leonard and the other Sons of the Pioneers' careers continued to flourish. Decca Records was the first to approach the boys about doing a few recordings. The band was promised a penny for every record sold. They gladly accepted the proposition and, in August 1935, stepped inside a West Coast studio to play four songs. One of those songs—"Tumbling Tumbleweeds" by Bob Nolan—would become the band's signature tune.

The Sons of the Pioneers' popular anthem captured the attention of studio executives at Columbia and Republic Studios, among others. The boys were asked to sing in a series of western films starring Charles Starrett and Gene Autry. Soon Leonard and the band were a preferred commodity, appearing in big-budget motion pictures as well as cowboy movies. They worked alongside such movie greats as Martha Raye and Bing Crosby.

By this time it had been close to two years since Leonard had met Arline while touring with his struggling band through the

Leonard and his first wife, Arline.

Southwest. Since he'd left New Mexico, the two had been writing one another continually and had fallen in love. When the Sons of the Pioneers were invited to perform at the Texas Centennial in 1936, all Leonard could think of was stopping by to see Arline on his way to Dallas. During his visit he asked her to marry him. She agreed, and on July 3, 1936, the couple became husband and wife. It was a simple ceremony held in Arline's parents' home.

Leonard and Arline waved good-bye to their families as they drove away. They were happy, hopeful, and excited about the wondrous possibilities that lay ahead of them. Their vehicle, loaded down with musical instruments and luggage, hurried off down the road and disappeared into the horizon.

Dale performing a number for the Chase and Sanborn Hour.

CHAPTER FIVE

Chicago to Hollywood

*Dale embodied the credo of the West as much
off-screen as she did on-screen.*
KATHARINE ROSS, *actress*

A well-dressed crowd
filled the tables surrounding the stage at the Chez Paree Theater
Restaurant in downtown Chicago. The Chez Paree hosted spectacular musical shows, featuring famous dance bands and promising
entertainers struggling to make a name for themselves.

The orchestra leader motioned to the musicians before him,
and they began to play. The enthusiastic night owls recognized the
tune and directed their attention to Dale Evans, gliding out of the
wings and following the spotlight to the center of the dance floor.
She began to serenade the audience with a song she had written
and had made popular, "Will You Marry Me, Mister Laramie? Will
You Marry Me Today."

Ray Bolger, the long, lanky dancer-comedian, tapped over to Dale and flashed an infectious smile her way. Dale sang and Ray, pretending to be Mister Laramie, danced to the music. At the conclusion of their act, the restaurant patrons erupted with applause.

Dale's voice and Ray's fantastic gyrations were well received at ballrooms, nightclubs, and hotels throughout the Midwest. Dale credited Ray with helping her find her niche in the market. He advised her to perform some of her original songs, "so people would think of you when they heard it." Previously she'd been lost in a sea of female entertainers singing the same ballads, but people responded favorably to her music and to her act with Ray. The success of "Will You Marry Me, Mister Laramie?" helped lead Dale Evans to the break she had been working toward. Bolger added levity to the song, pantomiming accepting her marriage proposal.

Before Dale's three-week engagement at Chez Paree, she had performed with myriad band leaders. From life on the road with Anson Weeks's orchestra to nightclub dates singing New Orleans–style jazz with Fats Waller, she had spanned the eastern part of the United States perfecting her trade. She had worked with some of the finest talent in the industry. Her dream of a Broadway career provided the incentive she needed to spur her on.

At the end of the Laramie number, Dale and Ray would hurry off stage. Returning moments later to take another bow, Dale would sing an encore if the audience was particularly appreciative.

The reception she received one night caught the attention of the head of the Columbia Broadcasting Network. Chicago station WBBM needed a staff singer, and Dale was offered the position. Her fellow employees referred to her as "That Girl from Texas," which was also the name of the program she would host there. Her duties at the station included work not only as a vocalist, but as an announcer and songwriter as well. She serenaded her listening

Promotional photograph used for Dale's jazz singing engagements.

audience with the popular melodies of the day, original songs she'd penned herself, and Spanish numbers for the large contingency of Mexican Americans who tuned in.

Dale Evans was fast becoming a recognizable name in the Windy City. She was sought after for public appearances and commercials. She auditioned to endorse a wide range of products from soap to car batteries. In one such audition she crossed paths with the Sons of the Pioneers. The first meeting between Leonard Slye and Dale Evans barely registered for either one of them, but a course had been charted for the two to meet again.

*E*arly in 1942 Hollywood agent Joe Rivkin wrote a letter to the 5-foot-2-inch, green-eyed, twenty-eight year-old Dale, requesting photographs of the ambitious entertainer. Rivkin had heard her sing on the radio and was impressed with her voice.

At first she laughed off the notion. She didn't think she had the "right look" for movies. It wasn't until a second invitation arrived that she took the idea seriously. The telegram she received read, "Paramount is looking for a new face for female lead in *Holiday Inn*. Bing Crosby and Fred Astaire to star. Joe Rivkin." The WBBM program director persuaded her to send Rivkin a few pictures. Dale reluctantly did so, believing the matter would be laid to rest once the agent saw the photographs. Three weeks later Rivkin sent word for her to come to Hollywood at once.

Dale descended the airplane steps and scanned the faces of the waiting people at the terminal window. She shaded her eyes from the bright California sun and rubbed her ears. The high altitude of the flight had given her a terrific head- and earache. Somewhere over Denver she had become nauseated, and although she had been on the ground for fifteen minutes, the color had not yet returned to her cheeks. Joe Rivkin would not catch her at her best.

She spotted the anxious agent pacing the tarmac. Rivkin's eyes studied the green complexion of the woman before him and frowned. "You certainly don't look like your pictures," he informed Dale. Still feeling ill, Dale followed the disappointed man to his car and the two hurried off toward Hollywood.

While en route to the studio Rivkin criticized her hair, nose, makeup, clothes, and weight. He listed the improvements she would need to make to secure a job in motion pictures.

Dale wasn't well enough to disagree with Rivkin's suggestions. He pulled his car up fast in front of the Hollywood Plaza where Dale would be staying. Any thoughts she had of lying down for a moment to calm her stomach were quickly dispelled. Rivkin led her to the hotel beauty parlor and instructed the stylists to "work their magic" on the suffering starlet.

Once Dale was coiffed and beautified, Joe took her to where the screen test would be filmed. His final instructions before introducing her to the casting director were to "lie about your age." Instead of twenty-eight, she was to say she was twenty-one.

The casting director assaulted Dale with a series of questions. Her answers were quickly interrupted by Joe, who stretched the truth on every occasion. Dale could tolerate such behavior only up to a point. When he told the director she was a talented dancer, she finally broke in. "Sir," she began. "I can't dance. I can't even do a time step."

Rivkin was furious with Dale. Her confession cost her the chance to be considered for the part in *Holiday Inn*. Impressed by

Dale's honesty and spunk, however, the director consented to give her a screen test to be used in casting other available roles the studio might have. Joe's spirits brightened a bit with the news.

Dale spent two weeks preparing for the screen test, and the determined agent monitored her every move casting the deciding vote on everything from audition scenes to the wardrobe selection. Dale's screen test included her singing a couple of standards, along with a short dramatic performance opposite actor Macdonald Carey. The stress of Joe's scrutiny of her every move finally caught up with her during the filming. She unleashed her frustration on Macdonald and when the scene called for her to slap the thespian she did so as hard as she could—leaving a handprint on the actor's face. She was mortified. At the conclusion of the filming, she was at her breaking point. She decided to confront Joe about the Hollywood experience thus far. She told him she wasn't going to be a part of any further deception—and that included being dishonest about her talents.

Caught up in the moment, she confessed to the stunned agent that she had a teenage son. Rivkin stared blankly back at his young protégée.

His mind reeling from the assault of information, Joe suggested that if Dale was hired by Paramount, she should keep the news of her son a secret. She steadfastly refused. Paramount Pictures rejected the entertainer.

Dale returned to Chicago, convinced that a career in motion pictures was not possible for her. The memory of the unsuccessful experience got lost in the daily routine of caring for her husband and son and singing engagements. Then, three weeks after she had left Los Angeles, Joe Rivkin phoned to tell her that Twentieth Century-Fox had seen the screen test and wanted to sign her to a one-year contract. Her pay would be $400 a week. The offer interested Dale. With that kind of money, she could put Tom through college when the time came.

"Send your teenage son away to school while you're out here," Joe advised Dale.

"If Tom can't come with me to Hollywood, we'll stay in Chicago," she firmly replied.

Rivkin was persistent and suggested that if she was adamant about bringing Tom with her to the West Coast she should tell people he was her younger brother instead of her son. The idea made Dale uncomfortable, but ultimately she decided it was a sacrifice she had to make in order to provide for her husband and son and realize her dreams.

So Dale Evans bade farewell to the Midwest and headed to Hollywood to begin what she hoped would be a lucrative film career. The studio executives ushered their newest addition to a variety of health clubs and salons. One was geared toward helping Dale lose a few pounds, another straightened and capped her teeth, and a third updated the style and color of her hair. She was given speech and elocution lessons and was required to do another screen test.

Finally, Dale was given her first starring role, and in a film that would give her a chance to show off her musical abilities: a college musical called *Campus in the Cloud*, a whimsical look at university life. Dale was thrilled with the opportunity, and slowly the reservations she had about the motion picture industry began to vanish.

On December 7, 1941, the Japanese bombed Pearl Harbor. The start of World War II impacted everyone's lives and businesses. Twentieth Century-Fox decided that frivolous movies would now be inappropriate. *Campus in the Clouds* was one of the first films scrapped from production. Dale's big break was shelved.

53

With the war in full swing and service-men in need of entertainment to boost morale, the Hollywood Victory Committee and
the USO were formed. Some of Hollywood's most promising
stars—Marlene Dietrich, Clark Gable, Betty Grable, James
Cagney—began performing at military camps up and down the
California coast. Dale was invited to be a part of this program, and
she eagerly agreed to serve.

When he could, Robert would accompany Dale on the road to
various shows, playing piano and doing spot jobs for her act. Both
Robert and Dale had demanding entertainment careers that kept
them apart for long periods of time. The marriage was beginning
to suffer as a result.

Dale shared the stage with many types of performers: jug-
glers, actors, dancers and even western bands. While touring
Northern California, she crossed paths again with Leonard Slye
and the other members of the Sons of the Pioneers. The group was
a favorite among the servicemen and servicewomen.

Dale's film career faltered during the first year of the war, but
her singing career was thriving. Unfortunately, Joe Rivkin was
not available to capitalize on her success. Rivkin had joined the
army and was stationed in Texas. Without his help, Twentieth
Century chose not to resign Dale once her contract was up. In the
year she had been with the studio, she had appeared in only two
walk-on roles.

In addition to her professional struggles, Dale was wrestling
with personal problems. She and Robert were drifting further and
further apart, and Tom seemed distant as well. He had agreed to
play the part of her younger brother, but he wasn't comfortable
with it. The lie conflicted with the Christian values he had learned
in church and Sunday school. The issue struck a nerve with Dale.
She didn't like being deceitful, either—it left her feeling cold and

empty. She attended church every Sunday but failed to carry her faith with her once the service ended. She decided the time wasn't right to focus on God or redeeming herself in the eyes of her son. "Once I become successful," she promised, "I'll devote more attention to my son and my faith."

Dale concentrated on saving her fledgling career. A frantic call to Rivkin yielded the name of an agent friend of his. "Art Rush can get you back on the radio," Joe assured her. The prospect of returning to the radio sounded appealing to Dale. She always felt appreciated there.

Art Rush was a soft-spoken man with a strong Christian base. Before becoming a Hollywood agent, he had pursued a career in the ministry. He had a reputation for being honest and for representing many talented up-and-comers— including Leonard Slye. Dale and he met and formed an instant bond. Art agreed to take on the young singer as a client and in no time had secured an audition for her at NBC.

Dale landed a job at the network as a vocalist on the *Chase and Sanborn Hour*, starring Edgar Bergen and Charlie McCarthy. It was Charlie McCarthy who secured the position for her during the audition by whistling approvingly at the singer while Edgar Bergen gave a pleased grin. The shows producers offered her a contract within a few days of her appearance on the set.

Dale's return to radio was short-lived. After repeatedly spurning the advances of one of the network's executives, she was dismissed from the show. Discouraged and out of work, she phoned Art Rush. Rush's secretary told Dale that he was busy with another client. "He's heading to New York to handle some business for a cowboy with the Sons of the Pioneers," the secretary shared with her.

Dale was furious. When Art returned to Los Angeles, she decided to lighten his workload. "I figured since you don't have

time to properly aid me in getting my roller-coaster career straightened out . . . it might be best that we go our separate ways," she announced to Art.

Dale's new agent, Danny Winkler, knew her work from her days in Chicago. Two weeks after signing with Winkler, she was offered a one-year contract with Republic Pictures and was set to star in a musical called *Swing Your Partner*. She hoped this role would open a window of opportunity on the Broadway scene. To be a part of a big, sophisticated production like *Oklahoma* had long since been a dream of hers. As she rehearsed the musical numbers for *Swing Your Partner* with the show's stars, she smiled proudly. She was convinced working at Republic was a promising start.

Republic publicity photo of Dale in 1943 for Swing Your Partner
(opposite page).

Republic publicity photo of Roy.

CHAPTER SIX

The Rise of a King

*He's the man who made the maidens mourn when
they discovered he had been a husband for four
secret years. Louella Parsons was the first to share
the news about his marital status and Republic
studios was deluged with written lamentations of
disapproving females. He's the right kind of guy who
is first in the hearts of his country women.*

PHOTOPLAY MAGAZINE, *November 1941*

eonard peered through
the black bars on the giant gate leading onto the Republic Pictures
lot. He watched actors, stagehands, wardrobe people, and technicians zigzag from one studio to the next. It was organized chaos,
and the young entertainer from Ohio wanted to be a part of it. The
year was 1937.

He glanced down at his watch—past lunchtime. He'd been
standing at the entrance of the studio since early that morning. He
didn't have a scheduled appointment, and no amount of persuasion

could entice the dour guard to let him pass. Leonard stared down at his cowboy boots, desperately trying to think of a way to get past the strict sentry. At that very moment, he knew, acting hopefuls were competing to be Republic's newest singing cowboy.

Leonard had heard about the search the day before while he was at a hat shop in Glendale. A frantic man had burst into the store in search of a John Wayne–style Stetson. When Leonard asked him what he was so excited about, the anxious thespian had filled him in on Republic's quest. Gene Autry was the studio's current singing cowboy star, but it was common knowledge there were contract issues that called into question future pictures with the actor. Republic executives weren't about to let themselves be held hostage to Autry's demands. They were now looking for a possible replacement.

These days Leonard Slye was calling himself Dick Weston. He thought the name sounded a bit more rugged than the one his parents had given him. And he needed a rugged handle if he was to be taken seriously as a western entertainer. He was no stranger to the motion-picture business, having performed musically in a number of films with the Sons of the Pioneers. In addition to singing he had played minor roles in a couple of movies, acting alongside Bing Crosby and Joan Davis. Universal even granted Dick Weston a screen test at one time, but he didn't get the job with the studio. Executives felt he photographed too young.

Leonard/Dick hoped the executives at Republic Pictures would see him differently.

The guard shot the desperate actor a stern look. Leonard smiled a pleading smile then, realizing it was having no effect, turned away. In the middle distance he spotted a group of studio employees returning from lunch. As they neared the gate, he decided to join them on their way in. Pulling his collar up and his hat down low, he slipped past the guard. The dedicated attendant spotted Leonard ten yards from the guardhouse and called out for him to stop. Leonard did as he was told. Just as he had resigned himself to being thrown off the premises, he heard a friendly voice calling his name. Producer Sol Siegel hurried over to him and shook his hand. The guard returned to his post when the producer waved him off.

Siegel produced many Gene Autry movies and had cast Leonard in minor roles in some of them. Leonard removed his hat and told Sol he had heard they were testing for singing cowboys. The producer nodded. "I've tested seventeen men already," he told Leonard. "And I don't feel good about any of them. If you have your guitar, come on in and give it a try."

Leonard serenaded Siegel with "Tumbling Tumbleweeds" and a fast-paced yodeling tune called "Haddie Brown." The producer was impressed and offered Leonard a screen test. Leonard floated out of the studio on a cloud, his hopes high that he might be offered a contract. There was only one hurdle to overcome for that to be possible.

The Sons of the Pioneers had become a popular singing group. Their public appearances, screen vocals, and radio programs had made the band a household name. Not only did the Sons appear on KHJM radio's show *Hollywood's Barn Dance*, but the boys were under contract with Columbia Pictures to provide music for its films. That contract was the hurdle Leonard needed to clear. Unless he found a replacement for himself with the band, he wouldn't be able to sign with Republic Pictures.

Leonard sought out an old friend of his named Pat Brady. Pat played the bass fiddle in a string quartet at a restaurant in Sunset Beach. He was an accomplished musician, and Leonard respected him, not only for his musical talents, but also because he hailed

Leonard and fellow band members not only supplied music for westerns at Republic, but for Columbia Studios as well.

from Ohio. Leonard invited Pat to take his place with the Sons of the Pioneers. "With you as my replacement," Leonard told him, "I would be free to test for the Republic contract."

The members of the band agreed that Pat would make a fine addition. Pat agreed to give it a try. Columbia approved of the replacement, and Leonard was free to leave.

On October 13, 1937, Leonard Slye signed a long-term contract with Republic Studios. He would be making $75 a week. The young boy from Duck Run, Ohio, had arrived.

Republic was known for its high-action B westerns. Herbert J. Yates, the president and chairman of the board of Republic Pictures Corporation, had entered the film business in 1910 by financing several Roscoe "Fatty" Arbuckle productions.

Yates had later developed the idea of the singing cowboy that helped make Bob Steele, Johnny Mack Brown, and Gene Autry popular. Indeed, Gene Autry was the studio's number one box-office draw among the western stars. Yates was not comfortable with his contract players having the power associated with celebrity, however. When Autry began making demands and seeking to make changes to his contract, the executive was determined to send the actor a message letting him know his status would not hold the studio hostage.

Yates decided to look for another singing cowboy—one who would help Republic increase its production of westerns and be ready to replace the veteran actor if necessary. Leonard Slye had no idea what lay ahead of him.

The studio set out to transform Leonard into "something the moviegoing public would like." After executives determined his upper body was undersized, he was placed on an exercise program that included one hundred handstands a day. Executives found a problem with Leonard's eyes, too. "They're too squinty," he was told.

For a time he used drops to relax the eye muscle and dilate the pupils. And then he received his first name change. Leonard Slye became known as Dick Weston, making his solo singing film debut under that name in 1937 in *Wild Horse Rodeo*, starring The Three Mesquiteers. Dick Weston also appeared in another film, *The Old Barn Dance*, opposite Gene Autry.

Leonard was grateful for the work and the chance to work alongside the Republic veteran. His weekly paychecks helped the young Rogers family purchase a home. The newlyweds were confident his big break was about to come.

In the meantime, however, another name change and image enhancement project was in the works at the studio. Herbert Yates and Sol Siegel decided to call him Roy Rogers. *Rogers*, after Will Rogers, and *Roy* because it was a name that rolled easily off the tongue. Behind the scenes, the publicity department was creating the quintessential cowboy biography for their newest acquisition.

Leonard Slye was amazed at all Roy Rogers had done. According to Republic Pictures, Roy Rogers was born in Cody, Wyoming, and grew up on a large cattle ranch. He was an expert horseback rider, bronc buster, and top hand with a gun and rope. After a time spent in New Mexico, he headed even farther west, parking his spurs at Republic Studios. The publicity department assured the reserved singing cowboy that altering history was what B westerns were all about.

For weeks, Roy Rogers sat around the studio lot waiting for his chance to be used in a picture. Six months after Republic completed filming *The Old Barn Dance*, production got under way for another Autry picture, *Under Western Stars*. By this time Gene and Herbert Yates had been at odds with each other for some time over the money Gene earned for radio appearances and endorsements.

Until their difference could be resolved and a new contract between them drawn up, Autry refused to show up for filming. Yates suspended the actor, and Roy Rogers was summoned to take his place.

Roy would be a good guy in this picture, starring opposite Carol Hughes and Smiley Burnette. The story revolved around a cowboy who takes on Congress to help save poor, starving farmers and ranchers during the Depression. Roy had learned to ride as a boy and was a natural for the role that called for an experienced horseman who would sport a white hat and ride a golden palomino named Golden Cloud. Smiley Burnette referred to the animal as Trigger in reference to his speed and style, and Roy instantly took to the beautiful horse with his flaxen mane and tail and proud arched neck. Trigger was four years old when Roy rode him for the first time. He had already appeared in one other movie, *The Adventures of Robin Hood*. He had an easy lope and fast gallop. Roy and he would become inseparable.

Under Western Stars premiered at the Capitol Theater in Dallas, Texas, in April 1938. Roy, Smiley Burnette, and the Sons of the Pioneers were on hand for the event. Roy and the band performed for the packed theater, and the town mayor gave the boys a key to the city.

In its review of April 12, 1938, the *Dallas Morning News* wrote, " 'Under Western Stars' introduces young Mister Rogers as a new cowboy hero, real out west and not drugstore variety. This lad isn't the pretty boy type, but a clean cut youngster who looks as if he had grown up on the prairies, not backstage with a mail order cowboy suit. An engaging smile, a good voice and an easy manner ought to put him out in front before very long."

Mattie and Andy Slye drove to the local theater in Duck Run to see the film. It was the first of many viewings. They followed the movie from town to town as it played in Ohio. Roy eventually had a print made for his proud parents.

The success of the film enabled Roy to help his family in ways he never could before. With his first paycheck he purchased a new brace for his mother's leg. It was something he'd always promised himself he would do if he ever broke into the business.

Roy toured the country for three months promoting the film. When he returned home he found stacks of mail awaiting him. Fans praised him for his easy manner, engaging smile, and good singing voice. They were equally taken with Trigger.

Trigger was owned by Hudkins Stables in Los Angeles. After visiting the palomino several times, Roy decided he had to have the horse for his own. "I knew they couldn't make anything better than this one," he told the handler. Roy paid $2,500 for his gold-colored costar. "It seemed a lot of money at the time," Roy later confessed. "But I can tell you for sure and certain it was the best twenty-five hundred dollars I ever spent."

Arline was happy about Roy's and Trigger's success in *Under Western Stars*. She helped him respond to the mountain of fan letters he received every day. The people who wrote him varied in age from eight to sixty-eight. Keeping up with the incoming mail was an expensive chore—one Roy and Arline paid for out of their own earnings.

The singing cowboy believed if someone was thoughtful enough to sit down and write him a letter, he had an obligation to answer.

Roy was eventually spending more in postage than his salary. He appealed to Herbert Yates to help him pay for stamps and possibly hire a secretary to help him respond to the writers. Yates said no, suggesting that Roy do what other stars do and throw the letters in the trash. Roy refused to do that.

Roy posing with numerous fan letters delivered to him daily.

To supplement his income, Roy arranged a series of one-night appearances. Theaters paid $150 for an evening performance. In between giving musical programs across the country, Roy continued to make movies for Republic, starring in films such as *Billy the Kid Returns*, *Days of Jesse James*, and *Red River Valley*. The fan mail increased as his fame grew. Still Yates refused to help Roy with the letters.

Frustrated with his apathetic boss, Roy rented a five-ton dump truck, filled it with fan mail, and drove over to the studio. He backed the vehicle up in front of Yates's office and dumped the letters on the lawn. Roy's actions prompted little response from the stubborn executive. He increased his star's pay by $25 a week but steadfastly refused to do more.

After two years with Republic, Roy Rogers was making $150 a week and spending most of that salary responding to fan mail. Agents sought the entertainer out, but it wasn't until he met Art Rush that he decided to trust his career to someone other than himself. Rush represented such talent as Nelson Eddy and Benny Goodman. He had grown up in Ohio and seemed to Roy to be a decent and honorable man. Rush arranged public appearances for Roy at rodeos and got him steady work on a radio show called *Manhattan Cowboy*.

In no time, under Rush's direction, Roy was earning ten times what his Republic acting job paid for his other appearances.

Roy and Arline set out to find themselves a new home, one that could accommodate the children they hoped to have. While searching for a new place, the couple came across a modest chicken ranch in the San Fernando Valley. Roy purchased the house for his mother and father.

Life for the Rogerses was happy. Roy's movie career continued to blossom, and Arline kept the home fires burning. They had everything they could imagine, except a baby. After several years of trying to conceive, the pair decided to consider adoption. Roy came in contact with many orphaned children while performing for group homes and hospitals. He knew firsthand the hearts that longed to have a home.

While on a business trip to Dallas, Texas, Roy took a tour of Hope Cottage, a home for orphaned, abandoned, and neglected children. Forty-two cribs filled one room at the facility. Each crib contained a baby. As Roy walked by the infants, his heart broke for their situation. His eyes settled on an alert, tow-headed moppet staring right at him.

The baby's name was Cheryl Darlene, and Roy knew the moment he saw her she would be his daughter. Arline was thrilled with her new baby. She had never wanted anything more than to be a wife and a mother. The couples's friends and family were thrilled for the couple as well. Some fans and newspaper columnists were less so.

It was not public knowledge that Roy was a married man. Studios, thinking a star's marital status influenced box-office receipts, wanted that information kept quiet. Now the whole world knew that Roy Rogers was a family man. The hearts of lovesick women carrying a torch for the cowboy were shattered.

Less than a year after Arline and Roy brought Cheryl home, Arline announced to her husband that she was expecting. The couple was ecstatic. On April 18, 1943, the Rogers brought home a second daughter, Linda Lou. That same year theater owners proclaimed Roy Rogers to be the number one western star in the country.

Not only was Roy Rogers a proud father and husband, he was now, according to Republic Pictures executives, King of the Cowboys.

Publicity still for the 1945 movie Don't Fence Me In.

CHAPTER SEVEN

Partners on the Celluloid Plains

I grew up with Roy and Dale on the silver screen.
They're heroes to me; they stood for everything right.
ROBY ROACH, *Los Angeles Times reporter,*
May 5, 2003

ale Evans sat alone in Herbert Yates's office. The owner and chief operator of Republic Pictures had requested the actress's presence, and, filled with nervous excitement, she had happily obliged. Yates had just returned from New York, where it was rumored he had taken in the Broadway musical *Oklahoma*. Dale had been told he was quite captivated with the production, and during her meeting with Yates, he enthusiastically described the play scene by scene.

"*Oklahoma* is a huge success," he praised. "One I would like to duplicate." She imagined he was going to tell her the studio would be making the film version of the show and they wanted her to play the lead. It would be a dream come true. What the CEO proposed instead caught Dale off guard. "Our Roy Rogers westerns are doing very well," he told her. "I think they could do even better if we had a female lead who could also do some singing. I think you're what we're looking for."

Dale stared blankly back at the executive, her mind reeling. *I sing in nightclubs, with dance bands, and on the radio—I'm not right for a western*, she thought to herself. "Are you sure you want me?" she finally asked. Yates nodded confidently. The less-than-enthusiastic expression Dale wore did nothing to change his mind. He informed her that the studio would be producing a Roy Rogers picture titled *The Cowboy and the Senorita*. "You're the Senorita," Yates concluded.

Left alone to consider the opportunity, Dale cast a dazed look around the room. She was under contract with the studio and could not refuse without serious reprisals. *I don't even know anything about horses*, Dale complained to herself.

By the early 1940s Roy Rogers was Republic's star and the number one Hollywood personality at the nation's box offices. He had been featured on the cover of magazines and invited to the White House to meet President Franklin D. Roosevelt. Dale recalled her previous encounters with the King of the Cowboys. "Years ago in Chicago, sharing a USO stage and an agent," she remembered.

Roy Rogers was Art Rush's client during the same period of time he represented Dale. She'd ended her relationship with Rush, believing he was too preoccupied with Roy's career. Now, in addition to the fact that B westerns were not the genre she wanted to work in, she was to be paired with a man whom she had been jealous of.

Her back against the wall, Dale decided to commit herself fully to her role as Ysobel Martinez. She felt that by delivering a stellar performance, Yates would be encouraged to cast her in better roles in better films. When she left the executive's office, she was convinced she had devised the perfect plan to end her career in western features.

Roy Rogers pulled his white Stetson hat low over his narrow eyes, shading his face from the hot Southern California sun. The set on the back lot of Republic Studios resembled an Old West town, complete with stagecoaches and livestock. Roy leaned against a hitching post and adjusted the six-shooters on his hips. Gabby Hayes, the Shakespearean-trained actor who had been Roy's sidekick in several films, stood directly behind him. Gabby wiped the sweat off his forehead with a red bandanna and scratched at the beard spread across his face. Roy glanced back at the rough-looking character and smiled.

Gabby grinned a toothless grin while watching a chorus of extras parade past, dressed in western costumes. Cameramen and lighting technicians scurried about, making the final preparations needed to begin the first day of shooting on Republic Pictures' production of *The Cowboy and the Senorita*.

Roy and Gabby hadn't met their costar yet, although they had been told that it was Dale Evans. "She started out as a singer, too," Roy told Gabby. "I've met her once or twice. I was a little too bashful to say much more than 'Howdy.'"

"Hope our leading lady is going to have a good time with this role," Gabby confided. "I've been saying all along the ladies' parts in these westerns have to be better. Maybe add a little romance, too," he chuckled.

Gabby wasn't alone in his thinking. The popular industry magazine *Movie Life* had recently conducted a poll indicating that the majority of theater goers wanted Roy Rogers's westerns peppered with a little romance. And indeed, Republic executives recognized the need to make improvements to their B westerns. Half of the movie audience was female, and they wanted to see women involved in the stories. They also wanted to see the King of the Cowboys kiss someone besides Trigger.

The swinging doors on the saloon down the dusty thoroughfare opened, and a beautiful woman with dark hair and a shapely figure exited. She was dressed in a Mexican gaucho costume, complete with a black, wide-brimmed hat. Both Gabby and Roy looked in her direction. "That looks like your Senorita, Cowboy," Gabby chuckled. "Can she ride?"

"Guess we'll find out soon enough," Roy said as he fidgeted with his spurs.

With the crew in place, director Fuzzy Knight began filming. Fuzzy called for quiet on the set, then gave the cue for Dale to spur her horse to the front of the general store, stop, and hop off. It was Dale Evans's first riding scene, and all eyes were on the capable-looking costar. On command the animal broke into a full gallop. Dale bounced around in the saddle as if she were on a merry-go-round and nearly fell off when the horse stopped. The director halted filming. Roy, Gabby, and some of the other crew hurried over to her, laughing. Dale giggled along with them. Roy and Gabby introduced themselves, and the three shook hands. "I can't remember seeing that much daylight between a horse and a rider outside a few rodeos," Roy kidded.

Dale had limited experience on horseback when she began making westerns.

Dale and Roy in 1944 from a scene from Song of Nevada.

Still laughing, Dale brushed the dust off her clothes, "I sing better than I ride," she said.

"We'll make a good team then," Roy responded. "I ride better than I sing."

By the end of the production, Dale Evans was a pro in the saddle. Roy Rogers commented to movie news reporters that she "never gave her work less than her all."

Dale Evans's acting job in her first film with Roy Rogers brought about the exact opposite response then she'd hoped for from Republic executives. *The Cowboy and the Senorita* was such a huge success theater managers petitioned Herbert Yates to team Dale and Roy up for another picture. By the end of 1944, the duo had made four more films together. The attention Dale received from fans and professionals alike helped her to see that this career move was for the best. Dale, Roy, and the other cast and crew members got along well. The object of Dale's jealousy had turned out to be a delightful person.

"There is nothing phony about Roy Rogers." She told *Movie Play Magazine* in 1945. "No hungry ego and nothing to prove. He has a job to do and he does it, sitting easy in the saddle; and what's more, he enjoys doing the work so much his attitude is contagious."

Roy's impressions of Dale were just as complimentary. In 1946 he told the same journal, "She is a person who always looks like she has just stepped out of the shower—real fresh and clean; and she is a good sport, too, carrying her weight in each and every scene and never complaining when she has to work long hours and do stunts that wear us out."

Roy and Dale followed up their hit *The Cowboy and Senorita* with *Song of Nevada*. Republic screenwriters duplicated the formula from the pair's first film—writing Dale's part to serve as a contrast to Roy's country ways. In *Song of Nevada* Dale played an uppity woman from the East who travels west to sell her deceased father's ranch and winds up crossing paths with a down-to-earth ranch hand played by Roy.

Audiences couldn't get enough of the on-screen mix of Dale's sass and Roy's patience. In one year Republic Pictures turned out seven of the popular westerns featuring their new stars. The day's work began at four thirty in the morning and continued until well after sunset. The cast and crew became very close. Indeed, Roy, Gabby, Dale, and the Sons of the Pioneers spent all their waking hours together. When they weren't filming, they were on the road performing at rodeos, country fairs, and theaters.

By the end of 1945, Herbert Yates proclaimed that not only did Roy Rogers continue to be King of the Cowboys, but Dale Evans was now the Queen of the West.

Everyone associated with the production of the Roy Rogers–Dale Evans movies got along very well. They confided in one another, and their husbands, wives, and children visited the set. Roy's wife, Arline, became great friends with Dale, and the Rogers girls enjoyed spending time playing in Dale's dressing room. During school breaks Tom would come by the studio lot to see his mother and end up talking with Roy and Gabby for hours. Years later, Dale would recall, "Making movies week after week, in the studio and on location—seeing the same familiar faces; listening to Gabby Hayes's delightful, funny stories . . . we became a family."

Professionally, Dale Evans and Roy Rogers seemed to be on a parallel course. Personally, their lives were quite different. Roy's home life was blossoming. He and Arline had a new home, two beautiful girls, and a third child on the way. In contrast, Dale's marriage to Robert Butts was ending.

A 1944 publicity photo for Lights of Old Santa Fe.

Over time Robert, too, had become busy developing his career. He was now scoring movies for Republic Pictures.

The notion of making their jobs secondary to their marriage was never considered. Their work schedules did not coincide, and they were leading separate lives. Divorce seemed inevitable.

In addition to her marital problems, Dale was tormented with guilt over the truth about Tom. As of yet she had not admitted to anyone in the Republic front office that Tom was her son. She ached to correct the public perception of their relationship. She was very proud of Tom. He was now an accomplished musician—writing, arranging, and conducting pieces for his high school orchestra. CBS orchestra leader Caesar Petrillo heard Tom perform a flute recital and told Dale that he had great promise. Dale wanted to do all she could to help Tom pursue his musical ambition.

After graduation, and much to his mother's surprise, Tom joined the army. His induction papers asked for the names of both his parents. He listed Dale Evans as his mother. When news reached Republic, the publicity executives hurried off to verify the claim. This time Dale told the truth. She was instructed to keep quiet about it. "We'll bury the story," she was told, but Louella Parsons unearthed it, revealing the secret to her audience in one of her radio reports. Dale was relieved that she could finally be honest about the matter.

*P*rivate information made public about either Roy Rogers or Dale Evans only seemed to endear them to their fans. Ultimately the pair created a total of twelve pictures together from 1945 to 1951 and were the number one box-office attraction in the world. Their individual talents enhanced each other's professional careers, and their friendship enriched each other's personal lives.

For a time it seemed the famous cowboy and cowgirl would ride off into a celluloid sunset and live happily ever after on screen. But their reign at Republic Pictures would soon be over. Storm clouds were looming in the horizon.

Dale in a scene from the 1947 movie The Trespasser.

CHAPTER EIGHT

Breaking Trail

*Dale Evans is a versatile work-horse of a
singer-dancer whose maternal sexuality
complements Rogers' boyish charm.*
PHIL HARDY,
The Western Film Encyclopedia, *1983*

erbert Yates sat
behind his enormous desk, puffing on a cigar. A cloud of smoke
hovered above his head before wafting out an open window. He
leaned back in his giant leather chair and concentrated on the frustrated actress in front of him. Dale Evans paced back and forth,
not yet saying a word. Finally, she arrived at the reason she had
come to see him. "I've done nine westerns for you, Mr. Yates," she
said firmly. "And you still haven't put me in a musical comedy." He
took another drag off his cigar as she reminded him of the promise
he had made her.

83

From the start of their association, Dale had made it clear that she wanted to perform in shows like *Annie Get Your Gun* and *Meet Me in St. Louis*. Yates kept promising Dale that he would put her in such a film if she would commit to doing one more Roy Rogers western.

Now her contract with Republic was coming up for renewal, and his offer remained the same. "After just one more Roy Rogers western," he told her.

Dale left the studio head's office prepared to quit. She had achieved a generous amount of attention riding the range with one of the most famous cowboys ever, but she'd had enough of the dust and tumbleweeds, gunplay, and getting fourth billing after Trigger and Gabby Hayes. "The heroine in a Western is always second-string," Dale told reporters with the *Los Angeles Times* in the fall of 1947. "The Cowboy and his horse always come first."

Audiences, however, felt her part in the Roy Rogers pictures was critical. When word reached the viewers that she was considering leaving to fulfill her stage ambitions, they flooded the studio with letters. One letter from the Roy Rogers Fan Club had three thousand signatures affixed to it.

Dale's appreciation for such support was not her only incentive to stay on with Republic. Yates threatened the entertainer with legal action should she choose not to fulfill her contract. Realizing such action might be too costly, she did as the studio asked. Before her contract ran out she appeared in ten more Westerns. But in 1946, afraid of being type cast and convinced she wasn't necessary to the success of the Roy Rogers films anyway, she decided to walk away from the popular franchise and Republic.

RKO Studios, one of Hollywood's premier motion-picture corporations, was set to film a grand musical featuring Eddie Cantor and Joan Davis. Upon hearing that Dale was available, they quickly signed her to play the role of the production's ingenue. The movie, *Show Business Out West,* was the type of sophisticated musical Dale longed to be a part of. It was to be her breakout performance.

$\mathcal{A}$lthough the title suggests otherwise, *Show Business Out West* was in fact a departure from the cowboy serials Evans was known for best. Her career had taken a new turn, but her marriage continued on the same old course. Dale Evans and Robert Butts divorced within months of her musical premiere.

Dale Evans's main focus had always been her career. The spiritual side of her life, which would eventually become the driving force in all she did, had not yet been defined. She knew the Lord had been gently calling to her, but ambition divided her attention. Dale's parents had been a strong Christian influence in her life. Her mother made sure her son Tom was raised in the faith. Over the years he'd grown into a dedicated believer. He proved to be a moral compass for his mother, agreeing to go along with the decision to keep their relationship a secret, but refusing to speak the lie himself.

"Christians don't lie," he had respectfully told her when he was twelve years old.

Dale and Tom had attended many Sunday services together over the years. Tom was very involved in the church's weekly activities. He used his God-given musical talent to serve. Dale admired his dedication and at times had felt the desire to honor the Lord with the skills he had granted to her, but could not bring herself to fully commit. Tom prayed that his mother would come to know the Lord as he had and that the desires of her heart would change. For now, however, Dale would continue to fill the void in her life with work.

*R*oy Roger's life was crowded with family, friends, and fans. By the start of 1946, he was one of the most famous men in America. Children and parents alike admired and respected the humble actor. Boys wanted to be him; girls wanted to marry him. Despite the fame and fortune, Roy never lost sight of what was most important to him. His daughters and loving wife were the light of his life. His world was lacking nothing, and just when the singing cowboy thought he was happier than he'd ever been in his whole life, Arline gave him news that added to his joy. The couple were to have another child.

Roy talked excitedly about the baby on the way in between shooting two more westerns for Republic. He shared his longing for a son with Gabby. "I'd like to have a boy," he told him. "Kind of balance things out on the home front," he added with a laugh. Roy got his wish. He and Arline did indeed have a son.

On October 28, 1946, the headlines scrolled across many major newspapers and emanating from the wire services read, THE KING HAS A PRINCE. Photographers flocked to the hospital to get a picture of the proud father posing with his namesake—Roy Rogers Jr. Mother and Father nicknamed their addition Dusty.

Roy with Dusty (opposite page).

Roy took time off from filming *Helldorado* to spend time with his wife and children. "There was no way I could remember dialogue while I was thinking of my new little fella," he later confessed. Roy stayed by Arline's side for several days. His excitement over the new family member was infectious.

After nearly a week of his round-the-clock hospital stay, Art Rush managed to coax Roy down from the clouds to venture outside. Art felt a round of golf would help ease Roy back to earth. But on the morning of November 3, Art's phone rang very early. His wife, Mary Jo, answered the call. The voice on the other end was broken, frantic, and unrecognizable.

She handed Art the receiver, and he tentatively asked who it was. "Art?" came the voice on the other end. Although the caller was crying and upset, he knew immediately it was Roy. "Arline is dead," he said. Art hung up the phone promising to be by his friend's side as soon as he could.

Roy's preparations for his golf outing had been interrupted by an urgent call from the hospital. When he arrived on the scene, he found his wife's room crowded with doctors and nurses. Arline had several tubes and wires hooked up to her body—she was pale and unconscious. She had suffered a massive brain embolism from a blood clot. Roy gently took her hand and stayed with her until the end. And then, almost as if in a trance, he left her room, phoned Art, and headed outside to wait for him.

Roy was in a fog as he exited the hospital. Tears filled his eyes and streamed down his face. He found his way to his car, and leaning against it, stared down at the ground, remembering Arline's peaceful expression as the nurse pulled the sheet over her face. Boys and girls on their way into the hospital with their parents noticed the grieving actor. With pen and paper in hand, they hurried over to Roy seeking an autograph.

When Art pulled into the parking lot, he spotted the forlorn cowboy amid a group of excited children. Through crying eyes he was scribbling down his name on the scraps of paper the children passed in front of him. As Art approached the group, he could hear Roy in a feeble voice wishing the fans, "Happy trails."

Almost as though sleepwalking, Roy drifted through Arline's funeral and burial consumed by despair. The question of how he was going to raise two little girls and a baby son on his own resounded inside his head. With the help of a live-in assistant Roy was able to take care of his children while maintaining a rigorous work schedule, but his low salary at Republic meant he was forced to take on singing gigs to help pay for the additional help his family needed.

He filled the void in his life left by Arline with volunteer work at children's hospitals. Entertaining terminally ill and handicapped children helped ease the pain of his broken heart. In the first year after Arline's death, Roy made more than 800 personal calls to sick boys and girls. His tireless efforts in helping so many youngsters while raising his own three little ones prompted the Boys Clubs of America to name him Father of the Year.

Jimmy Durante, the entertainer known for his long, bulbous nose, flashed Dale Evans an approving smile as she serenaded a studio audience with her rendition of "People Will Say We're in Love" from the musical *Oklahoma*. After months of waiting for production to begin on the role that was to change the course of her motion-picture career, RKO had scrapped *Show Business Out West*.

Dale took a job as the featured singer on the Jimmy Durante–Gary Moore show while waiting for the chance to be cast in another film. She enjoyed working with the comics, but was becoming increasingly discouraged with her agent's inability to secure her a part in a musical. Just when she was about to give up hope that she'd ever have the opportunity to achieve recognition as anything other than one of Roy Rogers's sidekicks, Republic Studios came calling again. This time the company offered her a contract to appear in a slate of dramatic features.

Dale signed for a second time with Republic and was soon in production opposite Doug Fowley in a film titled *The Trespasser*. Her part in this screen adaptation of D. H. Lawrence's book was a departure from her most popular film work to date. Instead of cowboy boots and fringe-lined skirts, she wore long gowns and was adorned in jewels.

Her character, Linda Coleman, was a young starlet romantically involved with a struggling middle-age musician. Reviewers were less than kind in critiquing Dale's dramatic debut, and the film as a whole did not fare much better.

Despite the disappointing reviews, Republic executives assured Dale they were looking for another project for her to star in. The fact that they still had faith in her talent was reassuring. In the interim she decided to embark on a singing tour and headed off to Atlantic City for her first performance.

The Steel Pier was packed on the night Dale Evans opened in 1946. Fans of the songbird's music and films flooded into the elegantly decorated club. Dale filled the stage with her captivating presence and inspired voice. Upon finishing her first set, she bowed to the applause of the audience and thanked them for their generosity. Staring out over the crowd before her, her eyes lit on two familiar faces in the front. Although dressed in a business suit, the trademark squinty eyes and handsome features left no doubt that this was Roy Rogers. Art Rush sat beside him, and the pair were cheering Dale's work. "It was like seeing friends from back home," Dale said. She hurried off stage and joined the pair at their table.

"I was in New York doing a show when I heard you were down here," Roy told her. "I talked Art into driving down to see you." The three talked excitedly, catching up on old times, discussing show business, children, and tragedies.

It had been two months since Arline Rogers had passed away. Roy had continued on as best he could, but behind the pleasantries and public persona was a lonely, dispirited man. Dale conveyed her sympathies again over Roy's loss. She reminded him of how much she'd always thought of Arline and offered to help in any way she could.

"The kids are doing nicely," Roy offered. "I just bought us a ranch near Lancaster, California. I call the place Sky Haven," he said proudly. Dale, for her part, bragged about Tom and his music career in the army. "He's a wonderful man," Dale boasted. "A wonderful Christian." Roy and Dale ended their long conversation with plans to meet the following night for dinner. She could tell Roy had something else on his mind he wanted to discuss.

The film duo spent a pleasant time together, eating and talking non stop. Roy had a lot to say about the welfare of his three children. He was worried about the effect time away from them was having. Dale could appreciate his struggles as a single parent. She had wrestled with the same concerns herself at one time.

Their conversation eventually shifted to lighter fare, and the couple reminisced about their days filming westerns. "The movies we did together were good," Roy admitted. "An awful lot of people liked us working as a team." After pausing for a moment he gently got around to the question that had been hanging over their meeting: "Why don't you come back?"

It was a kind, sincere invitation but one Dale felt she had to decline. She had graduated from saddles and sagebrush to serious actress and felt that the results of her efforts were just starting to be realized with the release of her first film. In her estimation more cowboy movies would only set her career back. Roy didn't press the issue. The two said good-bye and went their separate ways. Roy returned to California to begin shooting his twenty second western, *Springtime in the Sierras,* and once Dale's singing tour was complete, she went into production on a film called *Slippy McGee.*

Slippy McGee turned out to be an even bigger disappointment than *The Trespasser.* Making a successful transition from cowgirl partner to contemporary actress had proved nearly impossible. Critics were harsh, and audiences weren't attending the films.

Fans wanted Dale Evans to get back in the saddle again and ride with Roy Rogers. Republic was inundated with letters demanding she be put back in the westerns. The studio executives agreed that Roy Rogers pictures weren't the same without Dale Evans.

With two box-office flops to her credit, Dale was forced to reevaluate her career. Roy's generous offer to rejoin him in another series of B westerns intrigued her. After a lot of thought, Dale set up a meeting with Herbert Yates and told him that she'd like to "ride the range" again.

The first motion picture Roy Rogers and Dale Evans reteamed to appear in was *Susanna Pass.* The camaraderie on the set

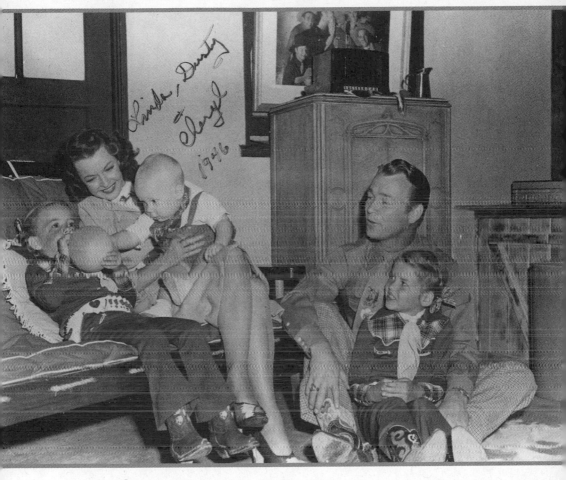

Dale visits Roy and his family in 1946.

among the stars, Gabby Hayes, and the Sons of the Pioneers was warm and loving. The mood of optimism and confidence the cast and crew possessed translated well onto the screen. Theatergoers turned out in droves to see Rogers's and Evans's latest film. By mid-1947 Roy Rogers was again among his field's top ten box-office moneymakers. Dale Evans had made the list as well.

Dale and Roy on their wedding day, December 31, 1947.

CHAPTER NINE

Cowboy King Marries Queen of the West

He used his immense talent to encourage moral and spiritual strength. Roy Rogers took the best of America's most important icon, the Cowboy, and created a code of honor for all. He was the most important American entertainer in the twentieth century.

MICHAEL MARTIN MURPHY, *singer-songwriter*

oy Rogers sat atop his chestnut-brown horse, Trigger, surveying the scene before him. His hand rested on his six-shooter, ready to draw on any villains planning an ambush. He'd spent the better part of the morning rustling up scoundrels who had been terrorizing local ranchers and townspeople. He would fire on any desperado—any bad guy lucky enough to have slipped by him who was now waiting behind a rock or bush hoping to waylay the cowboy.

Suddenly a tree branch snapped, and Roy whipped his famous steed around, his gun out of its holster and cocked. After a tense moment . . . a warm smile slowly filled his face. Dale Evans emerged from the brush on her horse. She eased up next to the cowboy hero, grinning from ear to ear.

"I thought you might have been one of the Monroe gang," he said.

"Sorry to disappoint you," she replied.

"Oh, I'm not disappointed," he concluded.

The two rode their mounts up a short incline. Although it was daytime, the trees covering the pass gave an effect of almost cathedral-like darkness. The sun filtered down through the leaves in gentle shifting patterns. Dale tenderly smiled over at Roy and sighed. The chemistry between the two was palpable.

In the near distance a director yelled "Cut!" and film crew members scurried about moving cameras and lights. Gabby Hayes meandered over to Roy and Dale as they dismounted their rides and discussed the scene. "That's the ticket," Gabby raved. "Audiences like a good romance."

Roy shrugged, looking unconvinced. "I'm not sure about this mushy stuff in a western," he confessed.

"What do you know?" Gabby kidded.

Dale and Roy exchanged a laughing glance. The pair respected Gabby's opinion but couldn't resist teasing him. Hayes was a former Shakespearean actor who, off screen, spoke eloquently. On camera his persona was that of a toothless, elderly curmudgeon. Out of the limelight Hayes was a well-dressed man who smoked a pipe and drove a black convertible. Over the years he had developed a life-long friendship with the King of the Cowboys and his costar.

Both credited the skilled thespian with helping them hone the craft of acting.

After Dale rejoined the western team in 1947, she, Gabby, and Roy were together a great deal of the time. Their schedules included not only motion-picture work, but also personal appearances at auto races and grand openings, as well as hospital visits to children's wards.

It was the stops at medical centers and orphanages that gave the famous players the most pleasure. Roy and Dale would sing for the kids, and Roy would offer them an up-close-and-personal look at Trigger and the pearl-handled revolvers he used in his films. He marveled at the strength and courage of the sick children he reached out to. They left the ailing boys and girls smiling and their spirits filled. Dale admired Roy's compassion for those in need. Roy appreciated Dale's generous nature and love for children. It was the most precious attribute they shared, and the catalyst for a blossoming romance.

As time progressed, Roy and Dale's relationship graduated from a warm, abiding friendship to love. Their contrasting temperaments fit each other perfectly. They enjoyed working together and sharing their concerns about their families and career aspirations.

Over meals at the end of an exhausted workday, the tired pair would lose themselves in conversation. One particular evening Dale touched on a subject that had been weighing on her heart for some time. "Do you believe in Jesus Christ?" she asked

"No," was his answer.

Dale had still not made her faith a top priority. From the age of ten, she had wrestled with letting God be the ruler of her life. The impact he had made on her son's life prompted her to examine her relationship with the Lord. She had learned of the sacrifices he

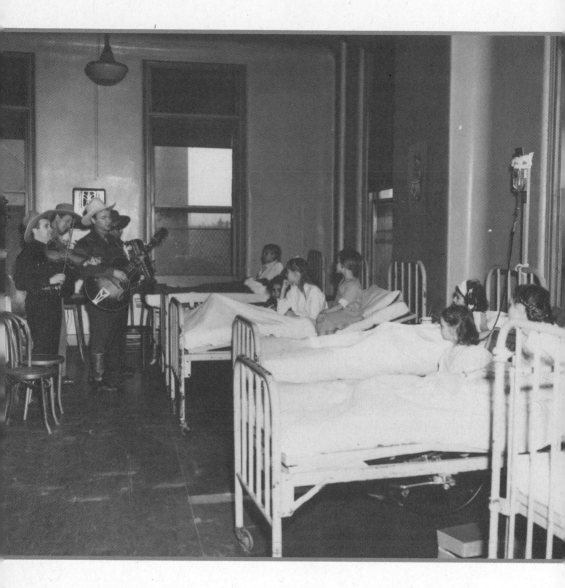

No matter how busy he was, Roy always took time to visit sick and hurting children in hospitals.

had made for her when she was a young girl attending Sunday school, and the thought of his dedication lingered in her mind. Somewhere in her heart she hoped Roy felt the same way.

His response to her question took her aback. "I can't say I do believe in Jesus," he reiterated firmly. "I've performed in too many children's hospitals," he went on. "If there is a God, I cannot understand how an innocent child can be born with a bad heart or crippled legs. I cannot understand the meaning of all those faces in orphanages. How can God let it happen?"

Dale was moved by the passionate way he spoke on the subject. It was obvious to her that he'd thought long and hard about this. His impressions had been shaped by the hurt he had seen and experienced for himself.

"If you can tell me why he lets children suffer, I'll go to church," he told her. Dale pondered his comments for a moment, searching for the right response, but nothing came. She was saddened by his feelings but didn't know enough about the Lord to counter his view. The pair agreed to table the discussion, unaware of just how much this theme would factor into their lives later on.

In October 1947 Roy Rogers, Dale Evans, and the Sons of the Pioneers ended an eight-week, cross-country tour promoting the film *Apache Rose*, in Illinois. Their last appearance before heading back to the West Coast was at the Chicago Rodeo. The stadium was filled to overflowing with excited fans of every age. Roy and Dale sat on their horses waiting to be introduced. Their rides were anxious and restless, as though they sensed this program would be like none other in which the pair had performed.

The couple shifted their attention from concentrating on the rundown of the show to the lion and tiger act performing in the arena. Dale glanced over at Roy who seemed more nervous than usual. "I talked to the kids at home," he said.

"Everything okay?" Dale asked.

"Fine. They said to tell you hello." An awkward silence fell over the couple.

Roy shifted uncomfortably in his saddle. "They love you, Dale," he added. "And so do I. . . ."

Unable to speak for a moment, Dale watched him reach into his pocket and produce a small box. He lifted a beautiful gold ring out of it and asked her to hold out her finger. "What are you doing New Year's Eve?" he inquired.

Awestruck, Dale admitted she had no plans.

"Why don't we get married then?" he suggested.

A drum-roll sounded, and the lights in the arena dimmed. That was Roy's cue for him and Trigger to rush out of the chute and into the spotlight. The announcer introduced the singing cowboy, and he was off like a shot before Dale could answer his proposal.

The spirited entertainer spurred her horse into the arena at the appropriate time in the show. Music spilled out of the overhead speaker as Dale took her place beside Roy. The crowd cheered and applauded. Dale looked over at Roy, smiled, and nodded. The music swelled, and the twosome launched into song.

Roy on Trigger.

*B*efore the announcement was made public, Dale insisted on discussing the idea of getting married with all of the children. Roy assured her that his young ones would accept her, but she wanted to be sure. Cheryl was seven and Linda was four when Dale and Roy told them they were thinking about getting married. They did not instantly respond, and Dale filled the pregnant pause with a question. "What would you like to call me if your father and I get married?"

Linda smiled approvingly and said, "We'll call you Dale." A loving embrace from the girls gave the soon-to-be bride the confidence she needed to begin making wedding plans.

Variety Magazine, along with KNNX radio, broke the news to the world in October that Roy and Dale were engaged. Disc jockeys repeated the date of the upcoming nuptials after each time they played Dale's new record—ironically titled, "Don't Ever Fall in Love with a Cowboy (He'll Love His Horse the Best)." For weeks leading up to the wedding, Roy and Dale were the subject of many newspaper columns and radio gossip shows.

Reporters speculated that Trigger would be the best man and that Dale's gown would be a red velvet cowgirl outfit.

As Roy and Dale made preparations for their big day and life thereafter, every move they made was reported on in industry magazines and newspapers. News that the couple had purchased a home in the Hollywood Hills appeared in *Photoplay* and *Life*. The articles were complete with pictures of their six-bedroom, six-bathroom house, once owned by fellow actor Noah Beery.

The spot Roy and Dale selected to be married at was the Flying L Ranch. Having recently completed filming *Home in Oklahoma* there, they felt the location was fitting. A number of journalists were on hand when the engaged pair arrived in Oklahoma City, near the site of the wedding, and bombarded them with questions about the ceremony. The curious lot wanted to know if Roy's fans would consider their hero a sissy for getting married and if their photographers could take a picture of the duo kissing. "We've never kissed in front of the movie cameras, so we're not going to start doing it for the papers, either," he told them. Newspapermen and newspaperwomen tagged along after the couple as they headed to the cattle farm, hoping to capture images of the simple country ceremony.

A furious storm had dumped mountains of snow on the six-thousand-acre ranch the morning of the New Year's Eve wedding. Family and friends staying at the homestead decorated the giant den where the vows would be exchanged. The bride and groom busied themselves getting ready and welcoming guests as they trudged in from the snowy landscape.

Moments before the ceremony was to begin, Roy was informed that the minister had not yet arrived. Deciding that the preacher might have lost his way in the blizzard or been forced off the road by ice, a search party was organized to look for the man. He arrived just as the group was heading out. After he took a few minutes to warm himself by the fire, the wedding began.

A string quartet launched into the traditional march. Roy waited at the altar with Art Rush beside him as his best man. The music played on and on, but Dale did not come down the aisle. The bride could be found in her room on her knees, praying. The severity of the situation had suddenly washed over her, and doubt held her captive. *Am I doing the right thing?* she asked herself. *With two unsuccessful marriages behind me, is it right to try again? Is it right for Roy? For his children?*

Feeling more alone than she ever had, she cried out to God. "You know who I am and what I am, Lord. You know the great responsibility I'm taking on marrying this man with three motherless children. Please help me be a good mother to Arline's children. Give me the courage and the understanding to establish a Christian home for them, a home like the one you gave me as a child."

She sat quiet for a time, letting the words of her prayer sink in. Moments later a deep sense of peace filled her heart. She knew God had heard her, and she knew she was ready to meet Roy at the altar.

Downstairs, the quartet had stopped playing the wedding march and were serenading the wondering guests with "I Love You Truly." Dale and her matron of honor proceeded down the aisle. When she saw that Roy was not waiting for her on the other end, she nervously scanned the room looking for him. Five minutes passed, and Dale was still waiting for Roy. Heads turned from the door to the bride. Finally, Roy and Art appeared, smoothing down their clothes and hair. Both were out of breath and smelled of smoke.

It wasn't until after the "I dos" were said and the reverend pronounced them married that Dale learned what had kept Roy. A cigarette butt, tossed in a wastebasket in the living room, had started a fire and engulfed the curtains. Roy and Art had raced in to put the blaze out and make sure the home was safe from any stray embers. Art summed up the day's activities best when he said, "What a way to start a wedding."

The Rogerses spent part of their first night as husband and wife sorting through cards and gifts from well-wishers across the country. The majority of notes expressed the hope fans had for the couple's long life and marriage. But there were a few letters from brokenhearted young women who had held out hope that they could one day marry the singing cowboy.

The handful of dismayed fans weren't the only ones who had misgivings about Roy and Dale's union. "Our marriage is going to have an effect on the studio, too," Dale told Roy.

He took his wife's hand in his and smiled. "A lot of people will try to tell us what to do."

The couple watched the snow fade from the horizon and give way to the sun. They began their first full day of their fifty-two years together on January 1, 1948.

A trip to church with the Rogers family.

CHAPTER TEN

A Higher Calling

She was a godly woman. A godly woman who lived
the Golden Rule—Dale Evans blazed a happy trail.
NAOMI JUDD, *singer-songwriter*

ale Evans stood in
the entrance of her new home staring at the furniture and boxes
waiting in the foyer. The job of combining two households would
be a daunting one, but she and Roy were looking forward to it.
The Rogerses had spent the first few weeks of their marriage hon-
eymooning and traveling about Northern California, appearing in
parades and rodeos. Fans cheered the newlyweds and appeared to
enthusiastically approve of their union. Dale prayed their children
were just as happy for them and that the transition from single
living to a two-parent household would be smooth.

Dale sat down on a couch in the living room, amid the unopened crates and barrels, and kicked off her shoes. A framed photograph of Roy's children rested on top of a coffee table. She gently lifted the picture up and cradled it in her lap. Three pairs of innocent eyes stared back at her. "I'll do the best job I can raising you," she promised the youngsters.

Her heart was filled with love as she reflected on the children in the picture. Cheryl was the most outgoing of the three. She had honey-colored hair and bright brown eyes, and she was quite a talker. Linda was a lot like her father, quiet, but behind her sparkling eyes was a torrent of emotion. Dusty, the baby, was a happy boy, affectionate and always laughing. *They'll keep me on my toes, but I'm up for the job*, she told herself as she placed the photo back on the table. Dale wasn't naive. She knew there would be obstacles to overcome, but she was hopeful that they would eventually be one cohesive family.

Dale forced herself up from her comfortable spot and examined the placement of the furniture in the room. Deciding to rearrange a bit, she moved the couch out of the way and scooted an oversized chair into the open spot. Linda snuck into the room and intensely watched Dale change things around. Marching over to the couch, she looked up at Dale and frowned. "This isn't your furniture," she told her. "This is Mommy's."

Dale stood staring into the child's face, frozen, at a loss for words. She'd never anticipated this reaction. "Honey, your mommy has gone to heaven, and she doesn't need this furniture anymore." Dale gently explained. "So it's okay for us to use it."

Linda didn't say a word. She simply turned and went to her room.

Dale sank into the chair and watched the little girl disappear from sight. *I am up for this*, she reminded herself.

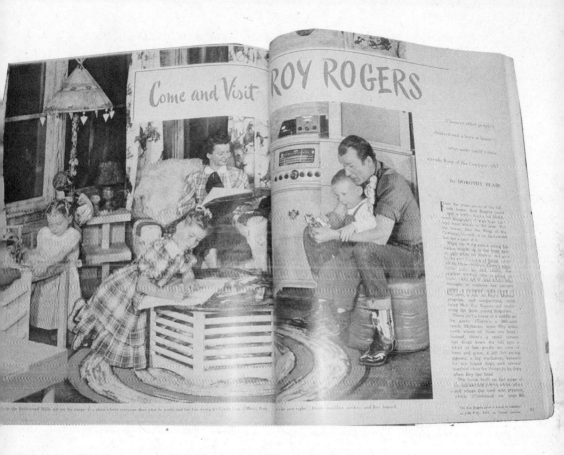

Magazine article about the Rogers family.

While Roy worked long hours at Republic Studios, Dale worked long hours at their home. Until she was to report to the next production, her job would be solely that of wife and mother.

She devoted herself to setting up house and trying to forge a new bond with Linda and Cheryl. The trail was a rocky one. Although the girls had initially been happy that their father was going to marry Dale, after the fact they were resentful and brooding. Dale understood that the response was out of loyalty to their mother. She felt her young stepdaughters' reaction was a natural one, and that with love and patience everything would work out.

One morning shortly after they'd all moved in together she sat at the kitchen table pondering her shaky relationship with her stepdaughters and rereading a distressing note from her agent. Studio officials had decided Dale would not be cast in any more roles opposite Roy. "Roy plays a strong, silent man of the West who never kisses his leading lady. Republic Studios thinks no one would believe it if you played opposite him now," Danny Winkler relayed.

Dale drew a cigarette out of a nearby pack lying on the counter and lit it. She was disturbed about the studio's decision, and so was Roy. She thought about the matter over a cup of coffee, finally coming to the conclusion that her focus would now strictly be on her new family.

She flipped the ashes off her cigarette just as Cheryl walked into the room. Dale smiled at the girl, but she did not return the favor. "I wish you didn't smoke," she chastised Dale. "My mother never smoked." The pretty seven-year-old didn't wait for Dale to answer. She simply turned and left the room. Dale put her cigarette out, tossed the pack in the trash, and vowed to never smoke again.

Just as Dale had resolved to be a full-time mother, however, the opportunity she had been waiting for came knocking. Danny greeted Dale with an elated "Happy day!" when she answered the ringing phone. Without pausing for Dale to return the sentiment, he blurted it out: "London producers want you as the lead in their production of *Annie Get Your Gun*," he told her. Dale didn't say a word. "Are you there?" he asked

*The Rogers family at home. Left to right: Roy, Linda Lou, Cheryl,
Dusty, and Dale.*

"I can't accept it," she heard herself saying. "Tom is getting married; the little ones have been exposed to chicken pox. . . . I couldn't possibly think of leaving. . . ."

Danny was thrown by her answer. "They need you right now," he added hopefully.

"I can't," she concluded. After a few more minutes of listening to her agent's attempts at persuasion, Dale said good-bye and hung up, deep in thought. Her commitment to her new family, however difficult it might be to handle at the moment, was her top priority.

At the end of each day, Roy would return home and the newly-weds would fill each other in on their days. Roy talked about the latest film production and the singing engagements he had coming up. Dale shared news about the children, confiding in him the trou-ble she continued to have with the girls. Some days Cheryl and Linda seemed to be adjusting nicely; others, they refused to eat, clean up their rooms, or go to bed. Roy was sympathetic but refused to take sides. "No matter how much it hurts," he told his bride, "I have to keep my mouth shut. Love and respect are things you can't force on anybody, much less kids. No one can win them over for you but you," he added comfortingly.

When Dale wasn't spending time with the girls and playing with Dusty, she was helping plan Tom's wedding to Barbara Miller, a talented young woman he'd met in college. Dale approved whole-heartedly of her son's decision.

Although she was always ready to give of her time and exper-tise, whenever Tom was around his mother he sensed she was preoccupied and worried about something. He knew things at home were hard and offered to listen to Dale if she wanted to talk.

Tom had been very supportive of Dale marrying Roy. Indeed, the two men had the kind of relationship she longed to have with Cheryl and Linda. After she confessed this to Tom, he suggested that she might find a way to reach the girls in church. He encouraged her to enroll the children in Sunday school and for Dale to attend a service. "Maybe God can lend a hand," he told her. "Why don't you come with me next Sunday?" Dale respected her son's opinion and decided to take him up on his offer.

On Sunday morning Dale helped ready the children and headed off to the Sunday service. The topic of the sermon was "The House That Is Built on the Rock." The pastor's message to the congregation about building a home on the rock of faith in Jesus Christ spoke right to Dale's heart. "A house set on a foundation like this can survive anything," the pastor promised.

The preacher extended an invitation that anyone whose heart was moved for the Lord could come forward to take him into their lives. Tom discerned the conflict in his mother.

She wanted to go to the altar and confess her sins, but pride held her back. He gently laid his hand on her shoulder and whispered into her ear. "Why don't you go?" he asked. "Give him your life and let him give you the peace you've sought for so long."

Dale shot Tom a defensive look. "I made that decision long ago," she snapped. "I've been a Christian since I was ten."

Tom's eyes filled with tears. He pitied her troubled soul. "Do you really know Christ?" he kindly probed.

The words of the sermon played over and over again in Dale's head. The conflict she felt at church followed her on the drive home. Glancing back at her three stepchildren, she ached to make things right, not only for herself, but for them as well. *I need time* *to think about thi*s, she said to herself. *Maybe next Sunday.*

Walking into the her home that evening, Dale was consumed with loneliness. Roy was on a hunting trip with friend, and she was unable to talk with him about the forlorn feeling she was experiencing. The emotion intensified until it overwhelmed her and drove her to her knees. In that desperate moment, with tears pouring down her face, she talked to God as she never had before. She confessed every sin and missed opportunity to be the Lord's servant.

She cried out to be changed. She cried out to be forgiven, and she bargained with God. "Let me live until next Sunday," she said. "And I will go down that aisle."

The following Sunday's sermon ended with the customary invitation for the lost to come forward. As the choir softly sang, "Jesus Gave It All," Dale Evans stepped out of the pew and hurried to the altar. A warm peace fell over her, and happiness invaded her being. It was as if a crushing burden had been lifted off her shoulders. Nothing would ever be the same for her or her family again.

Excited over the change in her life, Dale enthusiastically shared her experience with her skeptical husband. He was happy for her, but cautioned her about going overboard. Roy still questioned a God who could allow children to suffer. He would not easily be persuaded that the Lord was good. Even when he saw the miraculous changes in his own home as a result of God's love, he struggled with accepting the reason behind it.

Tom's suggestion had helped work a miracle for Dale. Her relationship with Cheryl and Linda improved tremendously. They prayed and sang hymns together, attended Sunday school, and memorized Scripture. Everyday they grew closer and closer. Now and then the girls would call Dale *Mom.*

Cheryl and Linda competed with one another over who would say grace before meals. With their heads bowed and hands folded, they would take turns thanking God for the food before them. Roy never said grace. With all the respect and sincerity she had, six-year-old Linda asked her dad why that was. "Don't you know how to talk to God, Daddy?" she inquired.

The question stayed with Roy for days. Unwittingly, his daughter had fanned an ember of belief burning in his soul. Linda's query, along with Dale's comment that "children don't imitate what we say; they imitate what we do," prompted Roy to consider attending church. *Someday*, he told himself.

In March 1947 the den of the Rogers' home was filled with show people, such as Pat Brady, Gale Storm, Andy Devine, and Smiley Burnette. Roy was hosting a party for friends, celebrities, and film crew involved in the production of another Republic western. The people on hand were drinking and smoking. Roy was giving tours of the home, and Dale was visiting with the guests. Those who knew her well recognized something different about her. She seemed to always be on the verge of blurting out some exciting news. One of Roy's costars couldn't help but ask about the change.

As Dale was explaining her new outlook on life and how her responsibilities had shifted from parties and fame to her marriage and children, Roy walked by.

The cowboy misunderstood her remark about responsibility and was quite irritated about the comment. He assumed she was complaining about how long the party was going on and passing judgment on the others in the room. "If you have a problem, this is no place to talk about it," he told her bluntly. He turned and walked away before Dale had a chance to defend herself. She choked back a tear, electing to cry out the hurt feelings over the scolding later upstairs in her room.

Roy and Dale were not speaking to one another the following morning. Roy stood by their bedroom window, thinking. His eyes fixed on the scenery and trees outside. Dale quietly dressed for Sunday service. She occasionally glanced over at her husband. Neither one of them knew what to say. Finally, Roy broke the silence. "If you're going to church I'm going with you," he told her.

Dale smiled and nodded. "That'll be fine," she replied.

Flanked on either side by his children and his wife, Roy sat in the middle of a pew listening to the sermon. From time to time Dale would sneak a hopeful peek over at him.

Toward the end of the service, she noticed that his head was down and his eyes were closed. The previous night's party had gone on rather long, and she deduced that he was tired from being up late.

But in fact Roy was not sleeping; he was praying. When the altar call was made, he lifted his head and sat bolt upright. "I'm going down there," he leaned over and whispered to Dale.

The King of the Cowboys was baptized the very next Sunday. He later told Dale that his decision to accept Jesus Christ as his savior came the very night the two had their disagreement.

"As I stood there looking out the window, it occurred to me that any financial provisions I might be able to leave my kids would someday be gone. The fame of being a movie star wouldn't last forever. I want my kids to remember me for something special, something that matters. I want them to remember me as a daddy who took them to church on Sundays and helped them learn how to live a good Christian life."

*B*y the time Roy and Dale were approaching their second anniversary, their blended family was thriving. The children were happy and healthy, and everyone was looking forward to Tom's wedding. They were prospering not only spiritually, but financially as well.

Roy had signed a new contract with Republic under which he received a 100 percent increase in pay. Dale was invited back to the studio as well. Executives had decided the married couple were not box-office poison after all and were planning to star them again in another series of westerns.

In addition their motion-picture work, the pair would be kept busy with another radio program, television appearances, and a long rodeo tour across the country. They would also make another album with the Sons of the Pioneers and a religious record for RCA Victor. Many of the songs they recorded were written by Dale. The success of their records inspired Roy to form his own company. Dale's tune "Aha, San Antone" became a hit, selling more than 200,000 copies. In November 1949 Roy Rogers and Dale Evans were the top moneymaking western stars in the country.

Dale pondered all these things and more as she watched Tom standing at the altar awaiting his bride. She was proud of the man her son had grown to be, proud of the Christian influence he had on her and the family. She was proud of her home, children, marriage, and the opportunity she and Roy continued to have to visit hospitals and entertain ailing children. *Truly we are blessed*, she thought to herself.

Tom and Barbara stood side by side exchanging their vows. Dale wept, remembering her boy as the baby she cradled in her

arms. The journey to this point had been a long one. She was excited for her son and daughter-in-law, knowing the wondrous adventure ahead of them.

"I wonder what God has in store for us next?" Roy asked Dale as the newlyweds marched out of the church at the end of the ceremony.

Dale didn't have to wait long to find out. A few months after the wedding she learned she was going to have a baby. Years before she had been told that the possibility of having another child without surgery was remote. Now she and Roy giggled happily when the doctor confirmed the pregnancy test.

News that the Rogerses were expecting was made public on February 1, 1950. Cards and letters from well-wishers across the country arrived at their home daily. Cowboys and cowgirls of all ages eagerly anticipated the arrival of the newest addition to the royal couple.

"Dear Roy and Miss Dale," wrote seven-year-old Sammy Finn of St. Joseph, Missouri. "My mom says you are going to have a baby. I hope it's a boy and that he will be best friends with Trigger and that he can help you fight robbers. That's what I would do anyway."

A 1949 publicity photo of Dale and Roy (opposite page).

Dale and Roy with Robin in 1950.

CHAPTER ELEVEN

Sleeping Angel

I believe with all my heart that God sent her . . .
to strengthen us spiritually and to draw us closer
together in the knowledge and love and fellowship
of Him.

DALE EVANS's *thoughts about the baby she and*
Roy shared, June 1954

 ale sat up in her hospital bed, nearly bursting with anticipation. She heard footsteps approaching her room and hoped it was the nurse bringing her baby to her. Dale's face fell when the nurse entered carrying a bouquet of flowers instead. The woman added the arrangement to the hundred that already filled the room. A young mother carrying a tiny bundle shuffled past Dale's doorway on the way back from the nursery. Off in the near distance, a baby could be heard crying. The nurse looked over at Dale and grinned. "Some little one sounds hungry," she said.

"It might be Robin," Dale offered.

The nurse smiled a troubled smile and started out of the room. Dale stopped her before she could leave. "Can I see my baby?" she asked.

The nurse walked over to Dale's bed and began fluffing the pillows and straightening the sheets in an obvious attempt to stall for time. "She's sleeping right now, Mrs. Rogers," she told her politely.

"I hope she sleeps this well at home," Dale sighed. The nurse continued to tidy the room as the happy mother shared with her the plans she and Roy and the other children had made for her homecoming.

"Are they going to let you take the baby home with you?" the nurse innocently asked.

Dale's face went pale. She had suspected something was wrong but attributed her misgivings to simply being nervous about motherhood. "Is there any reason why I shouldn't take my daughter with me?" she blurted out.

The anxious nurse studied Dale's face and suddenly realized that she had no idea what was going on. The nurse burst into tears. Dale stared back at her, overcome with worry. "I'm so sorry. I thought you knew," she cried to Dale. She ran out of the room before Dale could find out what the trouble was.

Frantic, Dale reached for the phone beside her bed and called Roy. "You said she was perfect!" she cried when Roy picked up the line.

To her mother and especially her father, she seemed flawless. When Roy bragged to Dale that their daughter had tiny little ears like her mother, he was unaware of just how sick the child was. When he looked into the cherub's face he saw perfection. Industry newspapers hailed the arrival of Roy and Dale's baby. Like Dale they believed the child was completely healthy: "Another little cowgirl was added to the Roy Rogers household yesterday when

Rogers' wife, Dale Evans, gave birth to a seven pound baby at the Hollywood Presbyterian Hospital. Both mother and the baby were reported in good condition," proclaimed the *Los Angeles Examiner* on August 27, 1950, for instance.

Robin Elizabeth Rogers was born on August 26, 1950. She was seven and a half pounds with blond hair and blue almond-shaped eyes. Roy learned the truth of his daughter's condition only hours before breaking the news to Dale. He hurried to the hospital after he hung up with his distraught wife to tell her about Robin.

The *Examiner's* report was only half right. Dale was in good condition, but that wasn't the case with Robin. She was born with Down syndrome, weak muscle tone, and a defective heart.

Both Roy and Dale collapsed into tears when he revealed that the prognosis for their daughter was grave. "They want us to put her in an institution," Roy told her. The overwhelmed Dale blinked away the tears. For the last nine months, she had been dreaming of carrying her baby home, rocking her to sleep and singing to her. Now doctors were suggesting she be sent away as if she had never been born. Seeing the hurt in his wife's eyes, Roy made it clear to the doctors that Robin would not be going anywhere but home with them.

Cheryl, Linda, and Dusty peered into the crib at their sister. They were fascinated by her petite features and sweet countenance. They took to heart the talk their parents had with them about her being a delicate flower who needed extra care and love. They promised to protect Robin and do whatever was asked of them.

After months of seeking help from doctors at prestigious medical clinics across the country and being told there was nothing that could be done for her medical condition, the Rogers finally accepted Robin's affliction. They decided to embrace the advice given to them by a pediatrician at the Mayo Clinic. "Shower her with love," the doctor told them. "Love will help her more than all the hospitals and medical science in the world." Roy, Dale, and the children would have no trouble doing that.

The Rogerses trusted this particular doctor's suggestion over any other's because they knew he had a Down syndrome child himself.

In those first months Dale wore herself out tending to Robin's every need. She hovered over the infant day and night. She held her constantly and never allowed the baby to cry for more than a moment because she was afraid the strain would affect her weak heart.

Through the difficult times and struggles to care for their helpless little girl, the Rogers family grew closer. Moved by the love Cheryl and Linda saw Dale showering on their sister, any lingering doubts that the girls had about their stepmother changed. Their hearts softened tremendously for the woman who tended to a sick baby, as well as three other children, a husband, and a career. Cheryl and Linda stopped calling her Dale, and began calling her *Mom* all the time.

It took some doing, but Roy managed to talk Dale into accompanying him on a personal appearance tour. He could see she was wearing herself out and needed a break. After hiring a special nurse, the two were off for a six-week trip through the Midwest.

As Los Angeles faded from view, the duo were quiet. They had many pressing matters on their minds. In addition to their preoccupation with home and family, there was a potential problem with Republic Studios brewing that needed their attention. The studio had decided to edit the films the pair had made and sell them to one of the three new television networks. Republic would profit from the venture but was offering nothing to the stars. Due to an exclusivity clause in Roy Rogers's contract, however—which stated that he retained the rights to his name, voice, and likeness for all commercial ventures—the sale of the pictures to television was blocked for the time. When Roy's contract was up with Republic, the studio thus decided not to re-sign the actor.

In the six weeks Roy and Dale were on the road, they traveled more than ten thousand miles and appeared in twenty-six cities. Then they headed home. Their problems with Republic continued, however. Now the debate over who had the last say over the B westerns being shown on television had been transferred into in court.

With Roy immersed in a heated battle with Republic, and subsequently freed from making any future films with the company, Paramount Studios offered him a part in a picture starring Bob Hope and Jane Russell titled *Son of Paleface*. Roy was cast as a government agent sent to find Russell, who was portraying an outlaw. Trigger had a part as well. Both were included to lend a touch of authenticity to the comedy.

The time spent on the set of *Son of Paleface* was a joy for Roy. Bob Hope and Jane Russell were true talents who made the experience of making the sequel to Hope's 1948 hit *The Paleface* a delight. Roy was so impressed with Hope's professionalism and humor that he penned an article about the actor called "The Reluctant Cowboy."

Once Roy completed filming he settled back for a rest with Dale and his children. The time off was short-lived, however—he and Dale began making plans to move to a bigger home in a drier climate. The couple felt Cheryl, Linda, and Dusty needed more space to run and play, and Robin needed to be away from the damp air and smog that surrounded the Hollywood Hills. The family moved to a handsome, sprawling Spanish ranch in the San Fernando Valley. They called their new home the Double R Ranch.

Dale devoted much of her time to her duties as mother, relishing every day she was on the job. She played the piano and sang with

Cheryl and Linda, drew pictures with Dusty, and nursed Robin, exercising her limbs and keeping her as comfortable as possible.

Roy Rogers's popularity was at its highest point ever. Hollywood reporters like Louella Parsons boasted, "If children were allowed to vote Roy Rogers would be President." To celebrate their popularity with the young moviegoers, Roy's handprints and Trigger's hoofprints were cast in cement in front of Grauman's Chinese Theatre—an honor reserved for the all-time film greats like Bette Davis and Clark Gable. After the ceremony Roy confided in Dale how flattered yet humbled he was by the event.

"Honey," he said, "who am I to be the beloved hero of millions of children? I'm just a hillbilly, an ignorant farm boy from Duck Run."

Dale kissed her gracious husband on the cheek and whispered in his ear, "No, you're something special."

Art Rush now represented Dale once again as well as Roy. In the early 1950s he decided it was time to bring his celebrated stars to television in their own show. The couple agreed that it was an idea whose time had come and gave their agent the go-ahead to set something up with a network.

Rush headed to New York to find a corporate sponsor for the program. Roy and Dale quickly assembled talent and crew to begin production on a thirty-minute pilot movie to be taken to potential supporters.

Dale was preoccupied through much of the staging. Robin was so frail; even the slightest noise upset her terribly. More visits to the doctor revealed that her heart was enlarged and worsening. Roy and Dale were told to prepare for Robin to die within six months' time.

A fast-talking radio minister recited a passage from the book of Psalms. Dale held her baby close to her as she adjusted the volume. The sun shone brightly through the bay window, bathing the room its warm rays. She sat down at the kitchen table and propped Robin on her lap. "Blessed is he who has regard for the weak; the Lord delivers him in time of trouble," the excited preacher read. "The Lord will sustain him on his sickbed and restore him from his bed of illness."

The message was in such contrast to the cold sense of desperation that tugged at Dale's soul. She stroked Robin's head, hoping somehow her baby understood what the minister was saying. "If only you could be restored from illness," she said, kissing the child's face.

Dale rocked the tired child to sleep while humming a soft tune. Just as Robin dropped off, she jotted the song down on a nearby pad of paper. Roy's radio theme music was a tune called "Smiles Are Made Out of the Sunshine." Not only did Dale feel the song wasn't western enough, but given all she and Roy had experienced she didn't think it adequately conveyed what it truly meant for a cowboy to ride the occasional bumpy trails. In three hours' time she completed the ballad that was to become the Roy Rogers–Dale Evans theme song:

> *Some trails are happy ones, others are blue.*
> *It's the way you ride the trail that counts;*
> *Here's a happy one for you.*
> *Happy Trails to you until we meet again . . .*

As Robin's health continued to decline, "Happy Trails" served as a testament for the way the Rogerses would live their lives.

Roy decided early on that "Happy Trails" would be the theme
of a series he and Art Rush had planned to bring to television. If
the court case that Roy had pending against Republic ended in his
favor, *The Roy Rogers Show* was ready to go on the air as soon as
possible. The format for the series would closely follow the story
lines used in the B westerns. The Rogers home, the Double R
Ranch, would serve as the primary location for the program,
which would feature Roy and Trigger, Dale, Pat Brady, Bullet the
Wonder Dog, and a cantankerous jeep named Nellybelle.

In November 1951 a Los Angeles judge determined that Herbert Yates and Republic Pictures had no legal right to sell Roy
Rogers's films to television. A restraining order was handed
down permanently barring the studio from releasing any of his
movies for that purpose. With the case over and the way cleared
for the television series to go forward, a deal was quickly made
with NBC to broadcast the program. *The Roy Rogers Show*
debuted on December 30, 1951. Roy and Dale's popularity in
motion pictures and radio translated well to the smaller screen.
By the end of the first season, the pair were reigning over yet
another medium.

*R*obin's feeble cries filled the quiet halls of the Rogers home late
one hot August night. Dale was crying, too, as she lowered her
feverish baby into a tub of ice water. The mumps the child had
contracted had turned into encephalitis. The swelling in her head
was unbearable. Her eyes pleaded with her mother to stop the
pain. Dale and Robin's nurse were doing all they could to make her

comfortable. Nothing seemed to work. Finally, exhausted from sobbing and hurting, she drifted into a fitful sleep.

Earlier in the day doctors had told Dale and Roy that their daughter's heart had undergone considerable strain; she couldn't take much more. The couple dozed off and on, stirring at the slightest sound. The family dog was restless as well, sensing something was wrong. He sat outside Robin's bedroom door whining.

The little girl's temperature continued to rise through the night, reaching 108 degrees before she lapsed into unconsciousness. The grieving parents stood over the child's bed watching her fade away. Dale blinked away the tears and cast a glance around the room at the beautifully wrapped presents for Robin's birthday party. She was a day away from being two years old.

At four o'clock on August 25, 1952, Robin passed away. She was laid to rest in her christening dress with a blue ribbon in her hair. "The hardest thing I ever did was look at my daughter in that coffin," Roy said later. "She looked like a small-size, sleeping angel."

As time passed, Roy and Dale's anguish subsided. Their hearts remembered the blessing their angel was and what wonderful lessons they learned from her short stay on earth.

"That little baby gave us a perspective we might never have found without her," Dale was able to say in 1993. "We needed her, more than we ever knew when she was with us. She brought a wonderful peace to our lives. . . . She smiled and our troubles fell away. She taught us patience and humility; and in the end, she showed us how to be of use to God."

Dale and Roy on the set of their NBC series The Roy Rogers Show.

CHAPTER TWELVE

Faith in a Storm

Today there are movies and television shows that I
wouldn't even let my horse Trigger see. Kids still
like to see the good guy win and the bad guy lose.
When the roles are reversed, as in many of today's
movies, kids get their thinking in trouble.
LOS ANGELES DAILY TIMES, *interview with*
Roy Rogers, September 15, 1976

oy Rogers rides hell-
for-leather on Trigger up the main street of an Old West movie set.
Extras for his television series stand on either side of the dusty
thoroughfare, watching the cowboy perform spectacular, dangerous
feats of horsemanship. The bright sun dances off the U.S. Forest
badge pinned to Roy's pocket and off the silver on Trigger's saddle.
Dazzling in the natural light, horse and rider personify the great
American cowboy hero. Dale rides in behind them, dressed in her
best, and Bullet follows her into the scene as well. The couple hop
off their horses, turn, and look into the camera.

"Well, Buckaroos, it sure was swell getting a chance to be with you. . . . " Dale waves to the viewers and steps out of the shot. Roy removes his hat, takes a step closer to Trigger, and bows his head. "Oh Lord, I reckon I'm not much just by myself; I fail to do a lot of things I ought to do. But Lord, when trails are steep and passes high, help me to ride it straight the whole way through. And in the falling dusk when I get the final call, I do not care how many flowers they send. Above all else, the happiest trail would be for you to say to me: Let's ride my friend. . . . Amen."

An efficient director yells "Cut!" and the cast and crew begin wrapping up the program. A few excited children, diehard Roy Rogers and Dale Evans fans, scurry out from behind a roped-off area and race over to their heroes, thrusting pens in front of the pair. Autographs are quickly scrawled on scraps of paper and returned to their excited owners. These boys and girls represent a handful of the 1.75 million registered Roy Rogers–Dale Evans Fan Club members in the world in 1953.

That fan base invested heavily in Roy Rogers–Dale Evans products; in addition to personal autographs they bought a variety of items embossed with the Roy Rogers brand.

Forty-seven manufacturers across the United States turned out more than 360 different items—from binoculars to boots. The success of the television show made the pair America's best-known and best-liked cowboy couple and increased sales for their merchandise tremendously. In a single year consumers purchased 408,000 pairs of felt Roy Rogers slippers, 900,000 lunch kits, 1,203,000 jeans and jackets, and 2 million comic books and records. Roy Rogers was second only to Walt Disney in sales and licensing.

During the first year after Robin's death, the duo found comfort in their children and an abundance of work. They divided their time among their family, taping their television show, voicing their

Roy with one of the hundreds of products he endorsed during his career.

radio broadcasts, cutting records for RCA, and touring with their rodeo. Roy Rogers's shrewd business sense, and Roy and Dale's combined wholesome image, generated $20 million a year for Roy Rogers industries. The Rogerses also ventured into the restaurant business, adding 600 eateries to their franchise coast to coast before eventually selling the chain to Hardee's Fast Foods.

Whenever there was a lull in the constant activity that was their lives, sorrow over the loss of their daughter overcame them. Dale ached for her child; at times the pain seemed like a great boulder crushing her heart. Roy struggled, too, but found great solace in reading his Bible and praying. After Robin's passing, magazine and newspaper editors had approached Dale about contributing an article on how she and Roy handled the tragedy. She wasn't ready to share such a personal experience with the public just yet but knew in time it might be beneficial. Still, Dale decided to work through her grief by writing privately about Robin's life. Between rehearsals and recordings, she captured her thoughts and feelings about her child on legal pads, envelopes, and napkins. She set the events of her daughter's life down solely for her own edification and that of her husband and their children. Roy respected Dale's decision to keep her feelings private for the present, but he chose to share the difference his faith had on his life in times of crisis the moment he was asked by evangelist Billy Graham.

Thousands of people sat shoulder to shoulder at Houston's Rice Stadium. They were all there for a Billy Graham crusade. Thirsty souls hung on every word the evangelist said. Roy Rogers sat behind the zealous preacher, waiting for his time to speak.

After a kind introduction, Roy stepped up to the microphone and waited for the cheering and applause to die down.

"The Lord has really had his hands full with me, but I'm grateful," Roy began. "You see, Dale worked with God to bring me something I had longed for all my life. Peace. Materially speaking, for years I had nothing. Then for years I had much. But I soon learned that having too much is worse than having too little. Nothing ever seemed quite right. I was restless, confused, unsatisfied. But the power of prayer, and the feeling of spiritual blessedness, and the love of Jesus have no price tag."

At the conclusion of Roy's talk, he waved to the crowd and thanked them for their attention and ovation. He turned to his seat on the dais and saw Dale standing there. She'd had a change of heart and decided it was time to share her testimony. She reached out for her husband's hand and gave it a loving squeeze. She was so proud of him; tears stood in her eyes. When it was her turn to speak, she told the audience about Robin's illness and of the shock and outrage they felt when they were informed of her condition. "God's love, his compassion, and unfailing kindness do not prevent him from shaping us in ways that at the time are painful indeed," she told the crowd.

"But the pain of the shaping is always matched by the Master Potter's skill in healing the wound."

Roy and Dale's appearance at the crusade helped them to begin healing the hurt, and their honesty about their grief further endeared them to the public. Dale continued to write about life with Robin and slowly came to see that her story could not be contained in a single article, but must be in a book.

With Roy's blessing Dale began the process of finding a publisher for the book she titled *Angel Unaware*. Roy busied himself with planning their upcoming performance at the Madison Square Garden World Championship Rodeo. Just how much their faith was influencing every aspect of their lives became evident in the preparation for their New York appearance.

*T*hree key members of the management staff at Madison Square Garden paraded into Roy and Dale's dressing room, all wearing worried expressions. Roy invited them to sit down and talk with Art Rush and him about what was on their minds. "We understand you're going to do a religious number in your show?" one of the men asked. Roy smiled and nodded.

The men shifted uncomfortably in their seats and exchanged serious looks.

"We've talked about this, and we're not so sure this is the proper place for that kind of music," the spokesman reluctantly said. Roy and Art listened patiently to their arguments against Rogers's choice in doing a religious song. The performance was sold out, and management felt that mixing anything of a religious nature with the rodeo show would be a financial liability. They were worried that people might want their money refunded. Even merchants who sold various Roy Rogers products were leery of bringing elements of their faith into the act. "I know you're still mourning the death of your daughter, and that this might seem like a good way to deal with that," the manager went on, "but this might offend some people." Roy said nothing. The men took another approach: Roy stood to net more then $100,000 for forty-three rodeo performances in twenty-six days—surely he wouldn't want to jeopardize his percentage of the gate receipts.

Roy wasn't dissuaded. His cool blue eyes were trained unflinchingly on the managers. The scene was reminiscent of one from a B western with the hero cowboy squaring off against the wealthy, influential landowners.

"Dale and I have talked this thing out," Roy said without smiling. "If we can't do our religious number, we won't go on at all."

The response threw the executives. It was uncharacteristic for Roy Rogers to take such a stance, but he believed it was the right position to take.

When the lights in the rodeo arena dimmed and the announcer introduced the King of the Cowboys, Madison Square Garden executives were nervous about the sold-out crowd's reaction. They could only hope the decision to give in to Roy's demands was not financial suicide. Spotlights flooded the stadium, forming a huge cross on the center of the field. A hush filled the audience. Roy's voice broke through the quiet as he walked Trigger out into the darkness and began singing "Peace in the Valley." The spectators were riveted to their seats during the performance, and once the song had ended Roy received a standing ovation. The cheers were sustained for a full three minutes.

Years later, in 1972, Roy told the *Dallas Morning News*, "I admit it's hard at times to be a Christian in show business. But I guess it's hard to be a good Christian no matter what business you're in. I happen to have been thrown into show business. It's a job. One doesn't always get to do just what he wants to do most, but he can usually find a way to make his life worthwhile if he wants to."

*S*itting in Central Park days after her performance at Madison Square Garden, Dale found herself disappointed, her faith slipping. Dale had shopped her book about Robin to several publishing houses and had been turned down by all of them. Roy encouraged her to be persistent, but she was beginning to question the entire pursuit. "It's a sad story that will make people cry," one editor told her. "People don't want to cry." Written as if Robin herself were telling the story of her life, Dale hoped the book would make readers aware that God's strength is found in weakness. "Why did you guide me to write this book, Lord, if no one is going to read it?" she asked sincerely. Holding her manuscript in her hands, she

Dale with Bullet the Wonder Dog in 1953.

prayed for God to confirm that this was something he wanted her to keep at. The sunlight assaulted her eyes after having them closed for a time in prayer. She shaded them with her hand and surveyed the landscape before her. The grounds were busy with office workers and tourists enjoying the outdoors. Dale spied a group of children running and playing in and out of the sunbeams that streamed through the trees. A little girl stood near them, but she wasn't watching the other children; she was watching Dale. The child was about six years old, and her features were consistent with those who have Down syndrome.

Her mother was standing beside her, with a face that seemed strained and troubled. Dale recognized the look. She wanted to reach out to the woman and let her know she empathized. "If only she knew what a blessing God has given her," she thought out loud. The mother and daughter joined hands and headed out of the park. Dale watched them until they disappeared from sight.

Believing that the little girl was the confirmation she needed, she continued the search for a publisher. After two more rejections, a publishing house agreed to print the manuscript. *Angel Unaware* was in bookstores by Easter 1953.

Dale Evans became a much-sought-after author once the book was in wide release, and the reviews were excellent. *Angel Unaware* became a best seller. Wrote the *Chicago Sunday Tribune*, "*Angel Unaware* is a message of hope and courage; awakening millions to a more sympathetic understanding of retarded children." And Norman Vincent Peale added, "It is a story to be read and cherished, not only by the countless youthful admirers of Dale Evans and Roy Rogers, but by mature people of all ages as well."

Dale Evans and Roy Rogers contributed all the royalties from *Angel Unaware* to the National Association for Retarded Children.

Left to right: Dusty, Dodie, Dale, and Sandy.

CHAPTER THIRTEEN

Adding to the Family

At Harringway Stadium in London some 40,000
children were on hand to see the King of Cowboys
and the Queen of the West. I heard them roar like
young lions and watched them bow their heads in
meek silence like lambs. I watched them powerfully
sway—towards good—I like to think by a cowboy
film star who preaches the cowboy code. "I'm the
happiest cowboy in Hollywood because five years
ago I found the Lord."

HEDDA HOPPER, Los Angeles Times,
December 19, 1954

undreds of people
flooded into a Hollywood television studio and took their seats.
Curtains were drawn across the set for the *This Is Your Life* television show, but that didn't stop the eager audience from carefully
watching for signs of movement underneath the closed drapes. A
recording of the program's theme music serenaded the crowd for a

few moments, and then announcer Bob Warren opened the show with thanks to its sponsors and an introduction of the show's host, Ralph Edwards. Edwards took center stage, bowed to the audience, and began the program.

Shortly after introducing Roy Rogers, who thought he was on the program to honor a friend in the ministry, he revealed to the entertainer that he was the subject of the broadcast.

Rogers was indeed surprised.

Tears stood in his eyes as he heard the voice of a young boy named Rusty reminding him of a call he'd made to Seattle. Rusty had been hospitalized and diagnosed with cancer and was defying strict orders by his doctors to eat the food served to him and get plenty of rest. Rusty's father contacted Roy, hoping that a word from the boy's hero might help the situation. Roy talked with the youngster and promised that if Rusty obeyed his doctor's orders, he could come visit him at his ranch and even ride Trigger. That was just the incentive the boy needed. True to his word, Roy did have Rusty as a guest at his home once he was dismissed from the hospital. A few years had passed since that event, and now Roy was reliving the experience with the healthy boy whose disease was in remission.

Rusty was just one example of thousands of children's lives Roy had personally touched. The telling of his life's story included anecdotes about friends and family and the things Roy had done for sick, lonely, and poor children. Edwards's narration of Roy's influence on his family and fans was emotional even for him.

When Roy was joined by his parents, Dale, and his own children at the end of the broadcast, Edwards was visibly moved by the outpouring of affection for the modest matinee idol. Ralph later shared that in all the years *This Is Your Life* was on the air, the single person whose life was most requested to be showcased was Roy Rogers.

Roy and Dale were always surrounded by children, whether it be their own or the world's. The couple said they often felt like babysitters. "Moms and dads can drop their kids off at one of our movies and be sure they won't see anything bad," Roy bragged. Even though Roy Rogers and Dale Evans were clearly beloved, though they had a devoted following, successful careers, and a loving family, they languished in moments of grief over the loss of their youngest child. Two months after Robin passed away, Roy felt it was time to ease their pain with another baby.

They were completing a series of one-night performances in the Midwest when Roy suggested adopting another child. "I just want Robin," Dale lamented. Roy missed their daughter, too, but he was convinced they needed to shower their affections on an orphan baby. While on tour in Texas shortly after Robin died, the couple had visited Hope Cottage, where Roy and Arline had once found Cheryl.

During their time there Roy and Dale had seen a three-month-old Choctaw Indian girl whose name was Mary Little Doe. They held the baby for a few moments, allowing themselves to be taken in by her big smile and big brown eyes. Roy suggested now that if Mary Little Doe was still there, they should adopt her. He phoned Hope Cottage and was told Mary had not yet been placed. Roy immediately spoke for her. Mary's adoption went through quickly. By the time the paperwork cleared, Dale had come around: She wanted this baby so badly, she ached. Plans were made to pick up Mary after they finished their last show on the tour.

Roy and Dale happily prepared for their final performance, excited about the new little girl who would soon be in their lives.

The pair waited in the wings of the Gardens in Cincinnati, ready to make their entrance. Both were decked out in full western gear and greeted handicapped boys and girls with passes to meet the famous duo. Roy focused his attention on a frail-looking five-year-old boy dressed in a corduroy suit and a cap. He bent down in front of the lad and gave him his friendliest smile, extending his hand. The boy hesitated only a moment before giving Roy a hearty handshake and offering him a "Howdy, pad-nuh," in his best cowboy drawl.

Roy and Dale were instantly taken with the youngster. He had a spark that was undeniable. His foster mother told the couple that his name was Harry and shared with them his tragic past. He'd been abandoned twice and suffered from rickets and curvature of the spine as a result of malnutrition. His body was scarred with cigarette burn marks and poorly healed broken bones. After seeing the glow in Harry's face once Roy sat him on Trigger, the pair knew they had to have him for their own.

Roy and Dale returned to California with two new additions to their family. They called the baby Dodie and renamed Harry, John David Rogers, calling him Sandy for short. Linda and Cheryl took to Dodie and Sandy quickly, but Dusty was reluctant. He was six and quite suspicious of this "new kid" clinging to his parents. In time the boys became fast friends, keeping their parents on their toes at all times.

Sandy proved to be a wonderful companion to a spirited Dusty, who'd had only sisters to keep him company. They shared everything: toys, clothes, a room, and a penchant for mischief. Whether it was having dirt-clod fights with the kids next door, switching the mail in the neighbors' boxes, or stripping the rubber off the dashboard of their father's boat, they did everything together.

Roy spent hours with the boys, camping, fishing, hunting, and wrestling. The three would wallow around on the floor, bumping into furniture and occasionally knocking things off the walls. The boys carried on in the same manner when their father wasn't around, too. Dale would scold them and warn them to stop, but often they wouldn't listen to her.

One day in the fall of 1953, the noise in the Rogers home was deafening. Dusty had taken a running leap at Sandy, and the two had fallen backward over the couch in the living room. End tables and chairs lay on their sides or pushed out of place, and the floor was covered with papers, comic books, and magazines. The brothers giggled happily as they chased each other around, grabbing at one another's legs. "Enough is enough," came an admonishment from Dale down the hall. The boys halted only long enough to grab a few pillows off the divan and begin batting one another over the heads with them.

"Knock it off," their mother advised again.

"Aauugh! Aauugh!" shouted Dusty. Sandy repeated the sound, only louder, as the pair launched into a playful screaming match.

"I said stop it!" Dale urged her sons, her voice raised to be heard over their ruckus.

Sandy jumped on Dusty's back, and the two hit the floor with a thud. They rolled across the rug, leaving broken knickknacks in their wake.

KABLAM! KABLAM! KABLAM! KABLAM! KABLAM! KABLAM! Dale had raced into the room and fired a stage pistol, loaded with blanks, into the air. The sound reverberated throughout the house. The boys stopped in their tracks, petrified, afraid to make another move. "I said stop it," Dale whispered. Sandy and Dusty didn't say a word; they simply stared back at their mother, wide-eyed and nervous. Dale took a deep breath and, as loud as she could, shouted, *"Now be quiet!"*

Like a tough, no-nonsense sheriff from the Old West, Dale turned on her heels and sauntered out of the room. The siblings exchanged a terrified look and ever-so-gently took a seat on the floor. They decided it might be best to remain quiet for at least a few hours.

Depending on the individual personal appearances Roy and Dale committed to do, the spouses alternated keeping the home fires burning while the other was out. Wherever the two performed, they left a lasting impression on their audiences. Mixing their personal beliefs with their professional careers, they hoped to teach their children and their fans how to live in this world as Christians. It was a position many young admirers wrestled with.

Just before Roy performed at a rodeo in Houston, for instance, he received a letter from a boy who described the ridicule he was going through for following his beliefs. He told Roy that he liked to go to church, but some of his friends called him a "sissy" for doing so. After talking it over with Dale, Roy decided to answer the young man's letter publicly. Charlie Evans, a reporter from the local newspaper, was at the scene of the Sunday matinee when Roy addressed the audience and recorded the event in the *Houston Chronicle* for all to read:

> One of the best sermons we have ever heard was delivered Sunday. And it wasn't from the pulpit of a church. It

was from the center of the Coliseum rodeo area, delivered by cowboy star Roy Rogers.

At the Sunday matinee Rogers asked how many of the youngsters in the stands had been to Sunday school or church that morning. Then he advised, "All you little cowboys and cowgirls out there, be sure to go to Sunday school. You might hear some of your little friends say it's sissy to go to Sunday school. But don't you believe 'em. Going to Sunday school is the best way in the world to get started right in life," Roy told the youngsters.

When he had finished, we heard a couple of youngsters sitting next to us talking. "You see, we better start going to Sunday school again. Roy Rogers said for us to."

And we can imagine many others thought the same thing.

Roy and Dale's ability to reach children of all ages, and their worldwide fame, prompted Billy Graham to invite the couple to participate in an overseas crusade he was hosting. With Trigger in tow the pair set off for a tour of Europe to meet, minister to, and entertain the hundreds of thousands of fans they had across the ocean. The theaters were sold out before they left the States.

ROY ROGERS SHOT AND KILLED DURING LONDON PERFORMANCE. Art Rush reread the headline across the telegram. He swallowed a lump welling up in his throat. *It can't be*, he said to himself. He quickly made his way to the telegraph office aboard the *Queen*

Left to right: Dale, Linda Lou, Sandy, Marion, Cheryl, Dusty, Dodie, Roy.

Mary and demanded wires be sent to confirm the news. Art and his wife, Mary Jo, were en route to meet Roy and Dale in Glasgow when word of Roy's untimely death reached them. "There must be some mistake," he told his wife.

Several hours after receiving the first telegram, Art was relieved to learn the truth: During opening night Roy had been hit by birdshot cartridges loaded in one of the actors' guns. He and Trigger had been hurt, but not seriously. After the accident Roy rode to the microphone, blood streaming down his face, and addressed the anxious crowd. "They've been shooting at me for twenty years, and this is the first time they hit me," he joked.

Roy and Dale received warm receptions at every stop on the tour. Fans were on hand to greet them in England, Ireland, and Scotland. While the pair were in Scotland, they took time to visit children's hospitals and orphanages. Homesick for their own children, the trip was as much for them as it was for the ailing, lonely youngsters.

In Edinburgh the Rogers met and fell in love with a thirteen-year-old girl living at the Dunforth orphanage. Her name was Marion Fleming—a petite teenager with a fine singing voice. After she entertained Roy and Dale with an old folk song, the pair knew they had to have her as their own child. A few months and a fair amount of legal wrangling later, Marion became a part of the Rogers family. The couple relished their growing family. "We're either going to have to stop visiting orphanages or buy us a hotel to live in," Dale told Roy.

The Roy Rogers Show had become hugely successful. Every Sunday night at six thirty, families across America gathered around their television sets to watch Roy and Dale defend the town of Mineral City against cattle rustlers and crooks. With the help of good friend Pat Brady, his feisty jeep, Dale's dog Bullet, and of course Trigger, the Wild West was well on its way to being tamed.

In 1956 Photoplay Magazine proclaimed the program to be "America's version of a morality play." According to the same publication, more people saw one episode of The Roy Rogers Show than the film Gone With the Wind before it was on television. When asked why they felt their program was a hit, Dale responded, "It's our heritage. People in the East years ago moving West, searching out the West. There's something about the West."

On more than one occasion, the Rogers children joined their parents on stage at the opening or close of their televised broadcasts. Dressed head to toe in cowboy gear, Cheryl, Linda, Marion, Dusty, Sandy, and Dodie would race out of the wings to their parents waiting in front of the cameras. It was evident to everyone watching that there was an abundance of love in the Rogers family.

That sincere expression of affection, combined with viewers' love of the West, kept The Roy Rogers Show on the air for more than six years. Boys and girls everywhere tuned in for half an hour each week to ride the range with Roy and Dale and become a member of their family.

In June 1955 Roy and Dale brought another child in their home. She was a three-and-a-half-year-old little girl, half Korean, half Puerto Rican, with big brown eyes and short brown hair. World Vision, a Christian group that helps orphaned children in third-world countries, arranged the adoption of the child the Rogers named Deborah Lee. Roy and Dale were sure Debbie

The Roy Rogers Plan a Merry Christmas Roundup

By LOUELLA O. PARSONS
Motion Picture Editor
International News Service

IN THE big Dale Evans-Roy Rogers ranch house in Encino there will be an old-fashioned Christmas this year. Their six children—four adopted and Roy's own two—will gather around the Christmas tree which they will string with popcorn and cranberries and bright, shiny ornaments.

The happiest one in the group will be 13-year old Marion Fleming, the Scotch orphan Dale and Roy brought back from Europe after they heard her sing "Who Will Buy My Flowers?" in such a wistful tone that Roy told me he almost burst out crying.

Dale said, "We try to visit the hospitals and orphanages when we're on tour. This child we just couldn't leave behind. She was undernourished and had had three homes. She's gained 18 pounds since we've had her. Marion's best Christmas present came when we received a cable from Chief Constable William Merrilees in Edinburgh giving us permission to keep her with us and educate her. She is very talented and has already taught Linda Lou to dance."

"When I told her she could stay," Roy interrupted, "she threw her arms around my neck and said, 'This is the happiest day of my life, and all my wishes have come true!'"

But Marion is only one of the happy children who will gather

Conrad Mercurio

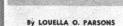 *Exclusive!*

DALE EVANS (standing at left) aids Linda Lou as Roy and Dusty look on. Seated are Dodie, Marion, Sandy. Cheryl was in school.

(Read Louella O. Parsons every day in the Examiner)

around that Christmas tree. In the Encino home, a-swarm with youngsters, is Sandy, 7, whom they adopted when he was a very sick child and who is perfectly healthy now; Doe, or Dodie as they call her, who is a 2½-year-old Choctaw Indian girl; Cheryl, 14 and a beauty, who is in school at Kemper Hall in Kenosha, Wis.; Dusty, or Roy Rogers Jr., 8, and Linda Lou, 11. Dusty and Linda are Roy's own children by a former marriage. Their mother died when Dusty was born, and he has never known any mother but Dale.

At luncheon, we had a chance to talk. I asked Dale how she manages with all those different temperaments.

"Oh, it's easy," she replied. "We have no problem with the adopted children. I just tell them I am adopted, too; that God is our Father and He chose Roy and me to bring them into our home. I ask the children whose real parents are living to pray for them because I feel they must need spiritual help to have given up their children."

After the death of their little daughter, Robin Elizabeth, both Dale and Roy became deeply religious.

She pulled a picture of little Doe out of her purse (both Dale and Roy carry pictures of all the children) and said, "Dodie filled a big void in our lives after Robin died. You know Roy has Choctaw Indian blood, so little Doe is very proud to say she is 'just like Daddy.' She is very talented; she sings, rides a horse and can outrun anyone I've ever seen."

To house this many takes a lot of room, but the Rogers have taken care of this. Their house has five bedrooms and there are four guest houses on the ranch.

"We have a watchdog that sleeps in the girls' bedroom," said Roy, "and he'd tear anybody to pieces who walked through their door."

"It must be a problem to feed that crowd," I couldn't help remarking.

"Not too bad," Roy said. "We raise our own beef, lamb, chickens, turkeys, and most of our own vegetables. Recently, I brought home some pigeons, and Dusty, who has become a Cub Scout, and the eight members of his troop are busy building coops to house them. They plan to raise the birds on their own."

There are no two harder working people in Hollywood than the talented and popular Roy and his equally talented and popular wife. They spent five months on tour this year and Dale says it's the last trip for her. She'll continue with Roy's radio show, but she doesn't expect to be on his TV shows. She's going to stay home with the children as much as possible.

"What will you do if Dale doesn't travel?" I asked Roy.

He laughed and said, "I'll tell you a secret. I'm staying home, too. Done all the traveling I want to do for a long while."

"Do your children realize you're the great Roy Rogers, or do they think of you just as their Daddy?" I asked Roy.

"Well, I can answer that with something that actually happened a few nights ago," he said. "Dusty and I were watching one of my old films on TV. Trigger and I were just about to get our man when Dusty yelled, 'Look, look, Daddy! There goes Roy Rogers now!'"

An article about the Rogers family written by Louella Parsons.

would be a delightful addition and a perfect companion for Dodie, who was the same age. Once Debbie learned to speak English, the two girls were inseparable. All was right in the Rogers home as the 1955 holidays fast approached.

A beautifully trimmed tree stood in the living room of the Rogers home, numerous brightly colored packages surrounding it, and seven stockings hung over the chimney. Lit candles ensconced with greenery were scattered about the festive holiday decorations. Everything was picture perfect and in keeping with all you might imagine the King of Cowboys and the Queen of the West's Christmas setting to be.

It was late at night when a candle on top of the television in the corner of the room began smoking. Burned down to nothing, the hot wick set fire to the TV set and quickly consumed it in flames. In a matter of moments, the fire spread to a nearby piano and burned through the floor. For the moment the Rogers family lay sound asleep upstairs, unaware of the potential danger.

Cheryl was the first to find the room on fire. She calmly phoned the fire department, then got her parents and the children up and out of the house. A light rain soaked the frightened family as they watched the firemen tackle the inferno. Before they could gain control of the blaze, the kitchen, living room, and dining room would be left in charred ruins. The family celebrated Christmas in the den. The smell of burned wood, slow-cooking turkey, and evergreen filled the air. Everyone was safe and well, and that fact overshadowed any inconvenience they had to endure.

Late in her life Dale Evans would tell *Yesterdayland Magazine,* "When I was a little girl I used to say when I grew up I was going to marry Tom Mix and I was going to have six children. And I really do think that I overdid myself, 'cause I married Roy

Dale with Debbie and Dodie.

Rogers. . . . I think big families are wonderful and together can withstand fire, flood, anything. We need more big families in this nation—where people band together in a common good."

Left to right: Dale, Dodie, Roy, and Debbie.

CHAPTER FOURTEEN

One More Hard Trail

The only things you can take with you are the things
you give away.

ROY ROGERS, Los Angeles Herald Express,
September 30, 1954

 xcited children scurried past cheery adults shuffling through the midway at the Canadian National Fair. The youngsters were so fixed on the coins in their hands and the games they wanted to play that they took no real notice of the grown-ups around them. Consumed with winning stuffed animals and other trinkets, they missed seeing the odd-looking man dressed in a fireman's uniform and cowboy boots, trying his hand at the ring-toss game. Among the families and young couples he seemed out of place—alone in his long beard and dark—glasses, but he drank in the sights and sounds of the fair as though there were nothing out of the ordinary about his manner of dress. On his way to the livestock area, he was approached by a pair of boys who saw through his disguise—it was the gold-tipped

155

boots that gave him away. Thrusting a piece of paper in Roy Rogers's face, the children asked him for an autograph. He happily gave them what they wanted.

In 1958 Roy Rogers and Dale Evans were two of the most recognized faces in America. Roy thought his outfit would give him a chance to see the fairgrounds without anyone knowing it was him. Diehard fans and hero-worshiping youngsters would not be fooled.

With the success of *The Roy Rogers Show*, the couple became more popular than ever before. Television was pervasive, and between their performances on NBC and at rodeos throughout the country, the pair were almost constantly in the public eye. Roy Rogers shirts, pants, boots, lunch pails, sheets, toothbrushes, and pajamas made it possible for followers to have their hero with them twenty-four hours a day. Such notoriety made it impossible for Roy and Dale to go anywhere in the United States or abroad without being found out.

On average Roy Rogers and Dale Evans were on the road performing twenty-two weeks out of the year. When school permitted, their children accompanied them on their travels. Working around the various schedules was no easy feat. Debbie and Dodie were in grade school, Dusty and Sandy attended a military academy, and Linda, Marion, and Cheryl were in high school.

The Rogers children often participated in their parents' act. Dodie and Debbie, three months apart in age, dressed like twins and did a sister act, and Cheryl, Marion, and Linda sang and danced. All of the Rogers children were paid for their work, which consisted of two shows a day. Roy and Dale deposited the youngsters' earnings into a savings account to be used when they got older.

When Roy and Dale were away from the family, they phoned home often. They spoke to each child and were updated on daily events. The siblings formed a special bond in learning how to share their parents with the world. The entire family was fiercely devoted to one another. Debbie and Roy were particularly close and had been since the day she'd come to be his daughter.

When Debbie had first arrived from Korea, she didn't speak any English. She was apprehensive about where she was going. She wore a fearful expression as she was carried off the World Vision airplane. Roy saw that she was scared and reached out his hand to her. She fell into his arms as though she instinctively knew he would keep her safe. Roy and Dale offered the same assurance to all their children. No matter what trials they encountered, they knew they could trust in their parents' love and loyalty.

Although Roy and Dale were individually recognized by various civic organizations for their parenting skills, no award came close to meaning as much to Dale as the card she received one Mother's Day from Cheryl.

> You came to live with us at rather a bad time, with Daddy so sad, and two little girls who were naughty, and a little boy who needed a mother's love that he had never known, and the youngest of those girls had for only three years. The older girl, when she was smaller, always kept her sorrows and problems in her, and even when you had problems of your own you were always there by our sides and you helped make our Daddy a Christian. I can't find anything fancy to say, but thanks from all of us and we really, really love you.

By 1964 Roy and Dale's television run had come to an end, and their time was spent almost exclusively doing personal appearances at state fairs, rodeos, and charitable programs. Dale kept up with her writing. Her books, published by Revell, were consistent best sellers. The spiritual records the two released were well

Dale and Roy perform at the Sheriff's Rodeo in Los Angeles.

received and were in constant demand at churches and crusades, but the motion-picture work the two had enjoyed seemed to be a thing of the past.

Since he'd gone up against Republic, other motion-picture companies resisted hiring the actor for film roles. Paramount Pictures had been the exception, but that was for only one film. Executives at all the major studios felt their ability to transform entertainers into stars gave them the right to control the product they created. The fact that Roy had successfully blocked Republic from selling his pictures to television did not sit well with filmmakers. Years after the dispute had been settled, Art Rush learned that every major studio in Hollywood had offered the help of its legal staff to Republic during the legal battle. As a result of Roy maintaining the commercial rights to his name and likeness, the industry brass had, in essence, blackballed the singing cowboy.

At the time Roy became aware of the backlash, he appealed to the Screen Actors Guild president, Ronald Reagan, for help. Reagan politely told him nothing could be done. Rather than dwell on the injustice of the situation, Roy decided to concentrate on other areas of his career. It was a move that paid off handsomely.

Rogers's chain of enterprises included his own television production studio, a company manufacturing and distributing western products, real estate ventures, a cattle and thoroughbred horse operation, a rodeo show, and a chain of restaurants. It made him one of the richest men in Hollywood. By the mid-1960s his personal wealth was estimated by some as close to $100 million.

Dale added twelve candles to the German chocolate birthday cake before her on the kitchen table. It hardly seemed possible to her that nine years had passed since Debbie had come into their lives. "All my children grew up too fast," she admitted out loud. Tom, Cheryl, Linda, and Marion were all married now, with children of their own. Dusty and Sandy were in high school, and Dodie and Debbie were about to enter their teenage years. "It seems like only yesterday I was draped in a Spanish costume and singing to the cowboy who would one day be my husband," Dale said as she pressed peanut brittle to the cake icing.

Roy would be absent from Debbie's twelfth birthday party. Years of galloping atop Trigger had damaged his spine and forced doctors to operate. On August 14, 1964, he entered the hospital and underwent nine hours of surgery to separate three vertebrae that had fused together. Debbie was consumed with worry over her dad.

Dale repeatedly reassured her that he would be fine. But it wasn't until the girl could see him after he'd been moved to a convalescent facility that she felt fully confident he would pull through.

During her visit with her dad, she told him about the shopping trip Dale, Dodie, and she had taken and showed him the stuffed animal she had won at Pacific Ocean Park. Roy smiled at his beautiful daughters, remembering them as toddlers sitting on his lap while he read books to them. After a moment of reflection, he wished Debbie "happy birthday" and told her to save a piece of cake for him. Dale, Dodie, and Debbie promised to do just that.

Dale lit the candles on the big day, and she and Dodie sang to Debbie. After she opened her presents, the three girls settled themselves in front of the television to watch movies and eat cake and ice cream. It was an evening Dale would relive in her mind over and over again.

Debbie had always been a generous child, sensitive to the needs of others around her; she went out of her way to help wherever she was needed. She was recognized by her school for her excellent service to community and outstanding citizenship. Dale was not surprised when her daughter came and asked permission to go to an orphanage in Tijuana with her friends from church. The mission would involve delivering presents to boy and girls who did without.

Dale drove to the church the following morning and watched her child board the gift-loaded bus. Debbie and her friends laughed and giggled as they waved good-bye to their parents.

Dale blew a kiss to her happy daughter and left to spend the day with Roy.

Roy's visit with his wife included an update on all the children and grandchildren. He asked about Debbie's trip into Mexico, and Dale told him how excited she was about it all. "She reminded me that we always let our kids choose the way they celebrate their birthdays," Dale shared with Roy. "She wanted this trip to be her present." Roy understood his daughter's heart and assured Dale she had done the right thing in allowing her to go.

A doctor stuck his head into Roy's room and delivered the good news that they were upgrading his health status from serious to stable. The couple breathed a sigh of relief as Dale kissed her husband's head. Neither of them could wait until he was home again and life could return to normal. Dale left the hospital feeling grateful for Roy's improved condition but preoccupied with all the activity in the Rogers household. She was uneasy about something and searched her mind to find the source.

The hot Southern California sun blasted through the front windshield of Dale's car as she headed home from the convalescent hospital in Bel Air. The notion that something wasn't right intensified the closer she got to the family ranch. A Bible verse leapt to her memory, and she recited it aloud: "My brethren, count it all joy when you fall into various trials, knowing that the testing of your faith produces patience. But let patience have its perfect work, that you may be perfect and complete lacking nothing. . . ." Dale's voice trailed off as she glanced at the hazy blue sky stretched out before her. She offered up a prayer of peace. For a moment her anxious heart was eased.

Dale pulled into the driveway and surveyed the welcoming sight of her house. Noticing Debbie's bicycle in the breezeway, she almost smiled. The red bike had been resting on its stand for a couple of days, but now it was lying on the pavement. The inclination that something wasn't right washed over her again. Ruth Miner, the family housekeeper, stepped outside and waited for Dale to get out of the car. Tears stood in Ruth's eyes as Dale approached the front door. Dale couldn't bring herself to ask what was wrong. "I have to talk to you," Ruth said, the tears sliding down her cheeks. Dale's color went white.

"The bus," Ruth said, her voice halting, "had an accident. . . . Debbie is with the Lord."

Dale stood frozen for a second, not quite grasping the news. "With . . . the Lord?" she repeated. Her knees buckled as she realized the gravity of the statement. "No! No! No! Not my baby!" she screamed. "Not again." Pain tore into her heart like a knife. She lashed out, tearing her clothes, pounding her fist, and wailing loudly. Ruth sobbed along with her.

In a fog from the tragic news, Dale rushed into the house wailing and beating the walls. "Why, Lord? Why my baby again? Jesus help me!"

Sandy and Dusty had arrived on the scene only moments before their mother. Debbie's death hit them hard as well. Sandy was too stunned to say anything. Dusty quickly deduced that he alone would have to help his mother through the initial hysteria. Dale collapsed into a window seat, crying. Sandy stood in the doorway of the living room, watching his mother fall to pieces, not knowing how to comfort her. Dusty finally broke in. He sat down next to her and tried to calm her down. He firmly grasped her shoulders in an attempt to bring her to her senses.

Shaking her, he said, "Mom!" Through tear-filled eyes she looked into her son's face. "Mom, for as long as I can remember, you've been telling me to trust Jesus. Now is the time for you to do that. Debbie is okay! She's with him!"

Left to right: Debbie, Sandy, Dusty, and Roy in Nellybelle
on the set of The Roy Rogers Show.

Dale thought about what he had told her and fought to regain some composure. He held his mother and gave her another moment to cry before convincing her she had to pull herself together. "What about Dad?" Dusty asked. "He's not strong enough to handle this. He's going to need you."

Roy's doctors broke the news to their patient. He was heartbroken. In his despair over Debbie's death he tried to pull himself out of his hospital bed. Tearing the IVs out of his arms and tugging at the brace around his neck, he cried out, "Why? Why her?" His physicians quickly sedated him and rushed him to the intensive care unit.

The grieving parents were almost inconsolable when information on how Debbie died reached them. She and another friend had been standing in the front of the bus talking with the driver when a tire on the bus blew out. The vehicle spun out of control and slammed into a station wagon. Six occupants in the station wagon were killed, along with Debbie and her friend.

The day after Debbie's passing, Dale visited Roy at the hospital. She sat beside him on the bed, neither of them knowing just what to say, both feeling the pain of another lost child. When it came time for Dale to leave, she had difficulty standing up. A glucose tolerance test revealed she was having a diabetes attack. Debbie's death had taken a toll on her health.

When Debbie Lee was laid to rest at Forest Lawn, devoted Roy Rogers–Dale Evans fans from around the world sent flowers to the funeral. Telegrams, letters, and cards expressing their condolences flooded into the Rogers home.

At the funeral Dale ran her hand across Debbie's dark hair and still face. She was wearing the same white dress she had worn at her sixth-grade commencement. Dale placed three red roses into her fingers as the tears dropped uncontrollably down her face.

A week after Debbie's service, Dale tried to go through her things. The grief once again overtook her, and she raced out of her daughter's bedroom. With her face in her hands she sat at the kitchen table sobbing, asking God for the reason why. This time it was Dale's mother who reminded her of her faith. "Frances," Betty Sue started firmly. "God's garden is the world, and his children are his flowers.

"He has a large mansion with many rooms. Sometimes he wants flowers for his mansion. Sometimes he picks a full-grown rose, sometimes half-opened. Sometimes a bud. He's taken a bud. Doesn't he have that right? It's his bud."

Roy and Dale agonized over the loss of Debbie for a long time. Dale wrote about their daughter in a book titled *Dearest Debbie*. Released in 1965, it paid tribute to the spirit Debbie brought to the Rogers family. Royalties from the publication went to World Vision International.

Roy with Dusty (left) and Sandy (right).

CHAPTER FIFTEEN

Soldier Son

Get a famous horse . . . gear your work toward
children . . . Nashville will resist the cowboy and
western music . . . do it with a passion . . . don't
overlook the impact of parades.
ROY ROGERS's *advice on how to become a cowboy*
star, June 1994

he Rogers home in Chatsworth, California, once bustling with children's activity, was eerily quiet by the end of 1964. Sandy was away at a private academy; Dusty was a junior in high school and always on the go; Dodie was the last daughter at home and involved in a variety of scholastic and social functions. Roy and Dale decided the 13,000-acre Double R Ranch was too big for their shrinking family and set their sights on moving to a smaller place in Apple Valley. The two talked about retiring from the entertainment business and living out their days in the peaceful high-desert community. "I'd like to do what I want to do," Roy told Dale. "Not what other people want me to do."

What Roy really wanted to do was open a museum. From the beginning of his career, he had held on to everything he thought could be included in display cases. Watches, saddles, cowboy boots, comic books, and fan letters were just a few of the items Roy had kept over the years. Inspired by Will Rogers's museum, Dale and Roy decided the time was right for them to open a place of their own.

After relocating to the Mojave Desert, the couple purchased a bowling alley, renovated the interior, and began unloading crates and boxes filled with western memorabilia. Their days of leisure would be spent visiting the museum, playing with their grandkids, breeding horses, and riding the dusty trails around their home on motorcycles. They limited their time in the public spotlight to guest appearances on television shows and Billy Graham crusades. Still, their schedules slowed only slightly after announcing they would retire. After more than twenty years in the business, the King of the Cowboys and the Queen of the West continued to be in public demand. The famous duo rarely refused an invitation to perform.

The Rogers family settled nicely into the Victorville Valley area. Dodie, Dusty, and Sandy were making new friends at school, forming bands, dating, and attending church. Sandy met a girl named Sharyn and fell in love.

He confided in his brother his desire to marry her and join the army. Dusty wasn't surprised by his vocation choice—as long as he had known Sandy, he'd had a love of the army. But he was only

Sandy (left) and Dusty (right) watch Roy do chores (opposite page).

seventeen and would need Roy and Dale's permission to enlist. Dusty reminded Sandy that he was still in high school and suggested he have a talk with their parents if he truly believed this was his calling.

Roy and Dale stared solemnly back at their son as he unfolded his plans for the future. Sandy had approached his parents once before on the subject. A year prior to this conversation, he had asked for their consent to enlist and fight in Vietnam. They'd refused because they wanted him to finish school. He was ready now with an answer to that argument. "I'm making good grades," he reasoned. "I want to serve my country. I want to prove myself a man. I promise to get my high school diploma in the service." Roy asked him about Sharyn, and, smiling proudly, Sandy told his father that she had promised to wait for him.

The determined teenager defended his position with sincere conviction. Seeing how determined he was to realize his dream, Roy and Dale relented and gave him their consent.

It had always been difficult for them to deny Sandy certain desires. He had come from such a tumultuous early childhood and dealt with his handicaps with the courage and strength of most grown men. As a result of the abuse at the hands of his natural parents, he had been left with poor coordination, astigmatism in one eye, and an oversized, malformed head. He was never physically as strong as most boys his age, but he enthusiastically fought to keep up, never feeling sorry for himself or discouraged. Roy and Dale admired him for his heart and tenacity.

Roy, Dale, and Sandy headed to the recruiting station, both parents doubting that Sandy could pass the physical examination part of the process. They believed they would be home later in the evening with their driven son by their side, prodding him to get ready for school. Military doctors ran Sandy through a battery of tests—all of which he made it through. At that point nothing stood in his way of being in the army.

In February 1965 Roy and Dale's youngest son headed off to basic training at Fort Polk, Louisiana. Dale would later admit to Roy that she had a premonition that Sandy would never be home again.

Sandy marched past the stands near the parade field at Fort Polk. Keeping in step with the other soldiers, he saluted the post commanding officers inspecting the recruits just out of basic. Behind his dignified expression was an overwhelming excitement. A look that seemed to shout, *I did it!* Dale was filled with pride watching her son in his dress uniform standing at attention awaiting words of encouragement from the fort's general. The captain of Sandy's outfit stood next to Dale; leaning over to the pleased mother, he said, "In my eighteen years' experience in the service, I've never seen a boy so anxious to become a soldier—never one who tried so hard." Tears filled Dale's eyes as she thanked the captain for his kind words. This was quite an accomplishment for a young man who had struggled to overcome abuse. At the close of the graduation ceremony, Sandy carried himself off the grounds like a decorated hero. To his mother, and those who knew of his trials, he was nothing less.

Sandy asked to be sent to Vietnam after basic but was instead transferred to Fort Leonard Wood, Missouri. By this time he had decided that a military career was his life's pursuit.

Throwing himself into his job as a soldier, he requested one of the most hazardous assignments in the army—working with the demolition squad. He was denied the duty because of his slow reflexes.

After a short leave and a visit with his family and fiancée in Victorville, he was transferred to Fort Knox, Kentucky. Prior to being stationed at that post, he had again put in for a tour of Vietnam, but was turned down for a second time. His slow reflexes were once more cited as the reason for the denial.

From Fort Knox Sandy was placed on a rotation headed for Germany. He would serve with the tank corps there. He was thrilled with the assignment. Dale flew to Tennessee to see her son off. Prior to his overseas trip, he confided in his mother that he'd celebrated his eighteenth birthday drinking with friends. Sandy's birth parents had been alcoholics, and although there had never been a need to suspect he might have a weakness for alcohol, Dale was now very worried.

She could see he was ashamed of his actions but reminded him that as a Christian he had a responsibility to act accordingly. She also reminded him of the responsibility he had for the girl he planned to marry.

Just before he boarded the military transport plane, he kissed his mother good-bye and promised her that he would stay away from alcohol. Sandy left for Germany, and Dale headed back to California.

Sandy wrote home frequently. His letters were filled with love and gratitude for his parents and their influence in his life. He wrote about the day-to-day experience of being in the tank corps. He worked hard and went from loading the vehicles to actually driving them, soon being promoted to private first class. He gave God credit for all his accomplishments and assured Roy and Dale he was more than happy with his life.

He kept in touch with his siblings still living at home as well. Dusty was in his last year in high school, and Dodie was in eighth grade. He encouraged them to "put their faith in the Lord because he's always around when you need him."

A giant harvest moon hangs over the great expanse of the plains. A rider in the far distance spurs his horse hard through brush and dried vegetation. The steed's hooves kick up loose dirt and gravel, making it next to impossible to distinguish the rider's features. As the horse draws close, he suddenly stumbles. After struggling to keep himself upright, the stallion falls hard onto the ground.

The rider is thrown. He rolls a bit then stops, lying prone and motionless. The horse picks himself up and hurries off, but the rider doesn't move. The bright moon casts a long shadow over the dead body. A loud scream fills the night.

In late October 1965 Dale sat bolt upright in bed, screaming from her nightmare. Sweat stood on her forehead, and she couldn't stop herself from crying or shaking the feeling that this had been more than a dream. Dale was in Texas visiting with her mother. She had wanted to celebrate her birthday at home and enjoy some time in the town of Italy. The people there had always made her stay special—inviting her to sing in the church choir and to give her testimony to the congregation. For Dale the time was always relaxing and rejuvenating. It gave her a chance to think things through with her mother and talk about God's great blessings. The nightmare stayed with her, however, clouding the trip with a sense of foreboding. The dream was still uppermost her mind when she returned to California. She relived it over and over again on the plane.

Dale stepped down off the aircraft at the Los Angeles airport and headed into the terminal. Cheryl and Marion were waiting for her. With one look at their faces, she could tell something was wrong.

Dale ran to meet her daughters. "What is it? Who is it?" she asked. Cheryl gently took her mother's hands in hers and stepped close to her. "It's Sandy, Mom," she said softly. "He's dead."

Dale's knees buckled and her body shook. Marion and Cheryl kept her from falling. "No!" she shouted. "Not Sandy! No!" She burst into tears, sobbing loudly. Roy and Dusty hurried to her. Tears stood in Roy's eyes. "He's in Germany, not Vietnam," Dale said to Roy. "How could another one of my babies be gone?" Dale buried her face in her hands and wept. Roy put his arms around his wife, and they cried together.

It took several minutes for Dale to calm down. Once she had, Dusty explained what had happened to Sandy. After twenty-six days of field maneuvers, Sandy and his company returned to their barracks exhausted and anxious for a break. The troops rested up and went out on the town on a Saturday night. Sandy was celebrating his PFC promotion at the enlisted men's club when some of the soldiers in his company talked him into drinking. In one evening he consumed half a bottle of champagne, two beers, four mixed drinks, and a sweet cordial. Sandy drank until he passed out. His friends got him on his feet, forced him to vomit, then put him to bed, where he collapsed unconscious.

In the middle of the night he threw up again; the next morning his companions found him dead. He had choked to death on his own vomit.

The Rogerses made yet another trip to Forest Lawn Memorial Park, this time to lay their son to rest. The military funeral was complete with a bugler playing "Taps" and a twenty-one-gun salute. The American flag draped over Sandy's coffin was neatly folded and handed to his grieving mother. His body was buried next to Robin and Debbie.

During this tragic time Dusty had received his draft notice and was scheduled to report for duty three days after Sandy's service. Roy appealed to the draft board for an extension. In so doing he found that the Sullivan Act, which prohibits the enlistment of the family's sole heir, reclassified his son to 4-A status. Dusty was exempt from serving.

*J*ust as they had done after Robin and Debbie's death, the Rogerses began the arduous task of going on minus another child. Sandy's death, no more than a year after Debbie's, left the family in a deep state of mourning. It did not, however, destroy their faith in God. Dale shared with readers in her book *Salute to Sandy*, "God has not promised us an easy way, but peace in the center of a hard way."

Neither Roy or Dale ever fully understood why Sandy was taken from them but rejoiced in the fact that he, along with their other children, had accepted Christ into his heart. Because of that truth they did not doubt that Sandy, Robin, and Debbie were with the Lord in heaven. Royalties from Dale's best-selling book and tribute to her son went to the Campus Crusade for Christ.

In the summer of 1966, the USO invited Roy and Dale to entertain the troops in Vietnam. Knowing how badly Sandy had wanted to be stationed there, they agreed to the tour in memory of him.

Dale and Roy entertain troops in Vietnam in 1966.

The western stars shared the stage with singer-comedian Martha Raye, western ballad singer Wayne West, and a country band called the Travelons. The show was well attended by homesick troops desperately in need of a distraction from the conflict. In addition to performing on stage, the USO troupe visited military hospitals, shaking hands with the wounded soldiers and Vietnamese children who had been caught in the crossfire.

Roy and Dale returned home after a two-week tour of one of the most volatile places on earth with a great sense of pride in American youth. They were sincerely moved by the strong, unbending dedication the troops demonstrated. The Rogerses felt the spirit of Sandy among those patriotic men.

During their travels they met with a friend of Sandy's who conveyed his sympathies over their loss. Dale asked the young man if Sandy had tried to be a good soldier. Without hesitating the friend replied, "Ma'am, he *was* a good soldier."

Roy and Trigger.

CHAPTER SIXTEEN

Rider in the Sky

It's been an interesting life. If you think practical,
you can make it through anything.
ROY ROGERS, *June 1996*

ays of early sunlight poured in through a large window, highlighting Roy Rogers's hospital room. The warm July morning revealed a pristine day under a cloudless sky. The fading eighty-six-year-old cowboy glanced around the room at his personal belongings. On a shelf next to a television were videocassettes of some of his western films and episodes of his television show. His cowboy boots waited near a tiny closet in which hung a fringed cowboy shirt and pants. He reverently studied photos of his wife and family smiling radiantly back at him in their best Sunday clothes. Among the pictures was a framed list of the Roy Rogers Riders Club rules.

The Riders Club was a group founded by Rogers for fans who wanted to follow in his footsteps. The club code was simple: "Be courteous and polite, protect the weak and help them, be brave, but never take chances, always respect our flag and country."

Roy lived his life by that code, believing firmly that "it's the way you ride that counts."

The cards and letters from well-wishers that filled the room were a testimony to how many lives Roy Rogers had touched with his heroics both on and off the screen. His loyal fans made him the number one western star for twelve straight years. From 1938 to 1957 boys and girls of all ages flooded into the country's cinemas to watch the ultimate good guy sing his way through danger, capture the heart of the girl, and triumph over evil. Roy Rogers was so popular and so well respected some of his friends in politics asked him to consider running for president.

If the test of a celebrity's greatness is his ability to win and hold a great mass following—Roy Rogers passed that test many times over. Twenty-three years after his last major movie had been released, audiences continued to seek him out and tell him how much they appreciated his positive influence and talent.

Roy stared out the window at the changing colors of the dawn sky, then turned to look into the faces of his children waiting at his bedside. They were worried and anxious about their ailing father. His body was weak, but his spirit was strong. When his time was up, he was confident about going to heaven.

It was his faith that kept his upbeat personality intact during his hospital stay.

Since the death of his son Sandy in 1965, Roy had decided to slow down. Throughout the 1970s and 1980s, he did so by making rodeo appearances, singing at Billy Graham crusades and the Grand Ole Opry, and doing guest spots on television shows like

Dale and Roy with Roy Clark on Hee Haw.

Hee Haw and *The Muppets* with Dale. He often joked that as far as he was concerned, he was a retired cowboy, but "nobody will let me get too far from the business." In the limited leisure time he had, he spent time hunting, racing his pigeons, and visiting with his children and grandchildren.

Roy knew he had been so richly blessed. From the early days of his career singing with the Sons of the Pioneers, to the last feature film he starred in 1975—*Mackintosh and T. J.*—Rogers's life's work had left a lasting impression on the public.

He'd had the great pleasure of being able to spend time with sick and orphaned children, travel the world, and speak out for the one who had given him so much. Indeed, to find the legendary cowboy minus his trademark grin was rare.

No doubt his partner on and off the screen could be credited with a great deal of the joy he had known for the last fifty-two years. Dale Evans was an energetic beauty who had captured his heart in 1946 and had been his constant through triumphs and trials.

"We both respect the other's desires," he once told reporters. "Dale knows what makes me tick. . . . I would be less of a man without her." The couple shared a deep love of children and family. Volume upon volume of books could be written about the life-changing effects they had on hurting and ill children languishing in hospital rooms and orphanages. A visit from the Rogerses lifted hearts and spirits of youngsters convinced they were alone and without hope. Such an impact prompted many physicians and hospital staff to refer to the pair as great humanitarians.

An American flag flapping in the breeze outside Roy's window caught his eye, perhaps reminding him of his love for his country. Throughout his career he had expressed his appreciation to be living in freedom and for the men and women who fought to make that possible. During World War II Roy had done his part to

Roy signs his name in a slab of concrete in front of Grauman's Chinese Theatre in April 1949.

support the United States. Classified as 4-A and prohibited from joining the military, Roy supported the troops by participating in countless USO shows and selling millions of dollars' worth of war bonds.

Roy closed his eyes, the sound of the flag popping in the wind lulling him to sleep. It was 4:15 A.M., July 6, 1998. He took a breath. The slow expansion of his lungs was accompanied by a deep sigh, and then he slipped quickly from this world.

Network and cable news stations announced the death of Roy Rogers around the clock. Documentaries about the cowboy, as well as his films, were broadcast continually. Extra editions of newspapers, featuring articles about his life and passing, were printed in cities and towns across his home state of Ohio and in Victorville, California.

In Rogers's memory California state senators and assemblymen adjourned for the day and flags were hung at half staff.

Within the first twenty-four hours after Roy Rogers died of congestive heart failure, the Roy Rogers–Dale Evans Museum received more than five thousand e-mails from fans around the world. Flowers flooded the lobby of the building, and mourners from as far away as Ireland came to pay their respects. Foreign dignitaries and U.S. politicians expressed their sorrow over Roy's death—making personal statements about the cowboy in interviews. Said President Bill Clinton, "I really appreciate what he stood for, the movies he made and the kind of values they embodied." Ronald Reagan added, "Rogers was a true American icon who delighted millions with his incredible ability to perform. Hollywood and the world will miss the talents of this legendary cowboy."

The halls of the Church of the Valley in Apple Valley, California, were filled to overflowing with sad followers of the King of the Cowboys. Roy "Dusty" Rogers Jr. spoke to those gathered at the public service and encouraged them to "look back on my father's career as a celebration of his life." As the mourners filed out of the sanctuary, they paused to comment on the life of the western star.

"He was more than a hero—he was everybody's friend," said fan Lorene Koch.

"He was the quintessential community icon," noted Bruce Williams, Apple Valley town manager.

At a private ceremony at Sunset Hills Memorial Park in Apple Valley, Roy's family and close friends stood around the grave site. Dale Evans, bound to a wheelchair since suffering a stroke, was led to her husband's casket, which was covered with red carnations. Her face was wet with tears as she added another flower to the mix.

Members of the Sons of the Pioneers sang "*Amazing Grace*" as Roy and Dale's children looked on, sobbing. A hush then fell over the grounds. The only sound that could be heard was the jingling spurs on the boots of the cowboys in attendance, and the snorting of a posse of horses nearby.

Butterflies drifted in and out of the pitches of light and shade of the lowering sun. The horizon range grew darker, tinted with rose and gold. It was the general consensus there that sunsets in Apple Valley would be even more spectacular now that Roy Rogers was a part of their beauty.

Dale holding the Holy Bible.

CHAPTER SEVENTEEN

Long Live the Queen

I do not feel that I am a writer. My books, inspired
by my experiences in life, have been the result of
God's guidance of my hand and mind.
DALE EVANS, Sunday Call Chronicle, *Allentown,*
Pennsylvania, September 20, 1959

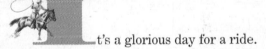

t's a glorious day for a ride. Dale squints as she looks up at the cornflower blue sky and the bright sun lighting the color so brilliantly. Roy is beside her, sitting atop Trigger. She is on Buttermilk, and the two are moving along at an easy canter. Dale smiles at Roy and sighs happily.

This was just one of thousands of memories Dale recalled about her life with Roy. She missed him with all her heart. As she lay in a hospital bed in her home in Apple Valley, she thought a lot of her husband and the times they had.

The year was 2000. Dale Evans was now eighty-eight years old and struggling with her health. Her days of riding fences long since past, she was grateful for the endless supply of memories about her life as Queen of the West.

She called upon those memories quite frequently now. Buttermilk had died years ago. Roy was gone, too. For two and a half years, Dale had been without her soul mate. "We were married for fifty-two years, a long time," she told a reporter shortly after Roy passed away. "He was a good guy. People liked him cause he was real. He wasn't flashy, he was just a real person." She couldn't help but fall in love with him, and she never doubted that they would be riding happy trails again one day.

Thunder from a storm brewing over the desert mountains shook the bright sky Dale could see from her bedroom window. If she could, she would walk outside and smell the clean air

Dale's book
My Spiritual Diary.

and rain on its way. Glancing over at her wheelchair, however, she was reminded of how difficult that would be. A heart attack in 1992 and a stroke in 1996 had left the cowgirl nearly immobilized. She was dependent on home health care nurses and her family to get her around.

Her stroke might have left her without the use of her legs, but it did not in any way slow her down. Shortly after Sandy's death she began hosting religious programs for the Trinity Broadcast Network and had continued to do so from her wheelchair at the age of eighty-eight.

She had also been able to continue writing for Revell Publishing. Her handicap was just a little inconvenience, in her estimation. Her faith and being able to write about its impact had been a constant in her life. Through joy, death, sickness, and disability she had been able to draw from God's source of strength, enduring many tragedies and gaining hope for the future.

She penned more than twenty spiritual books. Her work inspired many but sometimes baffled members of the entertainment industry who questioned the wisdom of being so vocal about religious beliefs. In 1953, when Dale was a guest on Art Linkletter's television show, her first book, *Angel Unaware*, about her daughter Robin's life and death, was a best seller. Linkletter asked her the question on many of his colleagues' minds: "What made you write this book?" Dale very candidly explained how God sustained her through the loss of her little girl. She wanted readers to know how he provides for us during our most trying times. Much to Art Linkletter's surprise, she went on to proclaim her faith to the show's studio audience and encourage them to meet the savior she trusted her soul to. Thousands of letters thanking Dale for her testimony poured into the show's producers.

An opened Bible sat on the nightstand next to Dale's bed, its pages well worn from a lifetime of studying the volume. She smiled as she looked over at the book, remembering what she'd once written about its message: "If we trust in the word of our Lord and Jesus and lift him up in praise, he will gird us with his almighty hand and help us through our trials." As she scanned the faces of her children around her praying, she hoped they would find solace in that truth. It was a truth she tried to convey in the song she wrote and recorded in 1955, "The Bible Tells Me So."

Many people, including her family, viewed her as the personification of goodness and saw her life as a shining success. Dale looked at it quite differently. She claimed the first half of her life was an unrelieved series of disasters, while the second half was a triumph over them.

Although Dale Evans recorded more than 400 songs, appeared in thirty-eight films, and recorded numerous television shows and radio broadcasts, she wanted most to be identified with Christian evangelism. She considered this aspect of her life to have been the "most meaningful and enjoyable." Longtime friends and fans knew her to be a strong witness who acted her beliefs.

"She was one of Hollywood's personalities who truly lived what she preached. She was a strong supporter of family and religion," said Dale's good friend Johnny Grant. Fan Pam Umbridge seconded that statement: "She suffered through the rocks and arrows life hurls at us with dignity and grace and without losing faith. I only hope my constitution is as strong should such calamities arise."

ROY ROGERS
KING OF THE COWBOYS
TRIGGER
SMARTEST HORSE IN THE MOVIES

My Pal Trigger

A REPUBLIC PICTURE

Of all the movies Dale made with Roy, her favorite was My Pal Trigger *in*
1946. She thought it was a marvelous human interest piece.

*A*mong the numerous awards and honors bestowed on the entertainer, she was most proud of being named California Mother of the Year in 1967. Looking over the faces of the loved ones around her, she recalled the challenges she'd endured that had brought her devoted family together. When she and Roy were first married, she'd questioned her ability to be a parent at all; now the Mother of the Year award was proof that she'd succeeded at it.

Dale is one of only a handful of entertainers who have three stars on the Hollywood Walk of Fame. One is for singing, another for acting, and the last recognizes her as Roy Rogers's partner

Former First Lady Nancy Reagan said "Dale was a true cowgirl through and through and an inspiration to millions, worthy of a dozen stars on the Walk of Fame." In 1995 Dale was indeed inducted into the Cowgirl Hall of Fame. Executives with the hall cited the impact she'd had on ambitious young women of the future.

Dale Evans died of heart failure on February 7, 2001. Fran Boyd, executive director of the Academy of Country Music, said that with her passing went "the last of the great ladies from a great era."

Her son Dusty said the secret to her success was in "living as though tomorrow would be her last day." She left behind sixteen grandchildren, thirty-three great-grandchildren, and a lesson in how to ride a hard trail.

Roy and Trigger.

CHAPTER EIGHTEEN

Golden Cloud

Trigger was gentle and kind . . . he had a great rein
on him as a cowpony. He was a fabulous horse.
ROY ROGERS, *1990*

giant full moon shines
down on a sleepy Mexican village somewhere in southern Texas.
In the shadows of a second-story balcony, Roy Rogers sneaks a
peek through one of the windows. Some of the territory's most
ruthless desperadoes have gathered and are making plans for a
bank robbery. Roy will go to great lengths to put an end to their
criminal behavior and bring them to justice. He'll need all the help
he can to get the job done, but for now it's just him and his reliable
four-legged partner.

After Roy learns what the bad guys are going to do, he inches
himself to the edge of the balcony and gives a soft whistle. Out of
the darkness, trotting into the beams of the moonlight, is a chestnut-
brown palomino. He waits patiently under the porch. After a few
moments Roy leaps over the railing and down onto the back of the
stallion. The pair ride off into the night, confident right will win
out in the end.

There wasn't a desperado who came up against Roy Rogers and his cohort Trigger who could escape the law. Trigger—or Golden Cloud, as he was originally named—began his movie career in 1938, appearing in the film *The Adventures of Robin Hood* as Olivia de Havilland's faithful steed. He appeared in a few other small-budget pictures before teaming up with the King of the Cowboys in *Under Western Stars*.

Trigger was the third horse Roy auditioned, and after giving the gold-colored pony a test ride, he knew he'd found the horse for him. The duo made eighty-six feature films and a hundred television shows together.

Billed as the "Smartest Horse in the Movies," Trigger could perform numerous tricks for the camera with no problem. He could count up twenty-five by stomping his foot, do simple subtraction and multiplication problems, drink milk from a bottle, and cover himself with a blanket. Roy and another trainer taught the horse self-restraint so he could enter hotel lobbies and hospitals to visit fans and patients. Trigger occasionally upstaged Roy during personal appearances, yawning or breaking into a dance step at the very moment Roy was talking or singing. Roy would often joke about "the ham in the horse."

Trigger paid a price for his fame. Whenever he made public appearances, some overzealous fans would pull hairs from his tail for souvenirs. At times Trigger's tail hairs were nearly all gone. While waiting for them to grow back, he wore a "tail toupee."

"No one sits a horse better than Roy Rogers," Dale Evans once said, "and no horse is as competent as Trigger." Indeed, Roy Rogers was the only cowboy star to make all his pictures with the

Trigger performs at a boys' residence home in 1951.

same horse. He was a superior animal who became one with his longtime rider, anticipating his every move and direction. Among the equestrian stars of the 1940s, Trigger was the best known, followed closely behind by the Lone Ranger's horse, Silver.

Images of Trigger graced innumerable lunchboxes, bedspreads, boots, and shirts. Boys and girls across the world treasured their precious memorabilia while pretending they were the King of the Cowboys galloping across the plains atop the golden steed. The highlight for fans lucky enough to see the pair in person was when Roy and Trigger would hurry to the center of the arena at the end of the show, and Trigger would take a bow.

Trigger was boarded at a ranch miles away from the Rogers home in Apple Valley. All of the family's show horses were boarded there. Trigger Jr., Trigger's successor, was born at that location as well. When Trigger was getting along in years, Roy rode the colt. Trigger Jr. wasn't as tall as Trigger, but he was just as smart.

By the time Trigger was thirty-three years old, his golden locks had faded to gray, and age was showing around his eyes and ears. He died in the summer of 1965. He had lived a long life and brought joy to the hearts of children everywhere. Roy was quietly despondent over Trigger's passing—so much so that he couldn't bring himself to tell his family. It was more than a year after Trigger's death before Roy broke the news to his children and the public.

Variety Magazine wrote on April 6, 1966:

> Trigger, Roy Rogers' famed Palomino, and his equine costar for many years, died of old age at thirty-three on July 3, 1965. It has just been disclosed by the film and television star that he is having the horse stuffed and mounted.
>
> Rogers rode Trigger in eighty-seven feature films and one hundred one half hour television shows. Trigger, Jr. and Trigger the third will attempt to fill the popular pony's horseshoes."

Trigger is on display today in his famous rearing pose at the Roy Rogers–Dale Evans Museum. Dale Evans's mount, Buttermilk, is beside him.

Roy with Trigger.

The Roy Rogers–Dale Evans Museum in Branson, Missouri.

CHAPTER NINETEEN

The Legend Lives On

There is no greater phenomenon in show business
than the individual and combined careers of
Roy Rogers and Dale Evans.
OAKLAND DAILY NEWS, *May 12, 1977*

The air inside the damp mine is stagnant and close. Roy Rogers hurries down a dimly lit corridor, occasionally looking back over his shoulder to see if the posse of outlaws he'd been one step ahead of has followed him into the pit. The coast is clear when he stops to inspect a suspicious section of mine. Lifting a nearby pick, he pushes it through a false wall in the cavern. The loose earth around it crumbles and a tunnel breaks open. He hurries through the jagged entryway and races over to a pile of rock in the corner. He inspects the large chunks of gravel and determines quickly enough that what he has in his hands is gold.

The cowboy will have to fight off a band of ruthless outlaws hoping to claim the wealthy mine for themselves before he can get to Dale and stop her from selling the property to a smooth-talking villain.

After a death-defying wagon ride and the exchange of several rounds of ammunition, Roy arrives just as Dale is about to sign the land away. He bursts onto the scene, his white hat gleaming. Dale smiles, relieved. She knew he'd come if there was trouble. She expected nothing less from the hardy, self-reliant, singing cowboy, and neither did the thousands of young fans who came to see him save the day.

*A*udiences made up of a variety of ages helped make Roy Rogers a box-office star, but America's love for western heroes began in the 1880s. Easterners, fascinated with life on the wild frontier, devoured dime-store novels about such characters as Black Bart and Billy the Kid. National magazines like *Harper's Weekly* were among the first periodicals to tap into the growing interest and hired artists and writers to cover the west. Their reports and drawings weren't always accurate, but readers seemed to prefer fiction over fact.

By the turn of the century, there was an endless supply of books, magazines, and plays dedicated to the cowboy. Zane Grey novels were extremely popular among young adult readers, and according to *The New York Daily News*, "most every home across the country has a copy of Owen Wister's western, *The Virginian*, on their night stand."

Not only was the cowboy popular in print, but he was immortalized in songs like "Git Along Little Dogies" and "Bury Me Not

A publicity still for one of Roy and Dale's movies.

on the Lone Prairie." In 1903 audiences flocked to theaters to see *The Great Train Robbery,* and the cowboy picture was born. The notion to combine a story about the hero of the sagebrush who sings country folk music did not come about until 1935, some thirty-two years after the first western was released. Three decades later moviegoers continued to be mesmerized by the Old West and the theme of good winning out over evil.

Republic Pictures was the front-runner in the western genre, committed to producing the very films ticket buyers sought. In 1934 Republic's Mascot Studios, under Nat Levine, made the first singing cowboy film titled *In Old Santa Fe*. Audiences embraced Republic's movies, and the studio reigned supreme for more than ten years. Out of this era came such western heroes as Tom Mix, Gene Autry, and Roy Rogers. Rogers became the most recognizable singing cowboy of the time. In 1948 an estimated eighty million people went to see his films.

*R*oy Rogers was viewed by millions to be the ultimate good guy—admired for being able to sing and use his fists. "When he and Dale square off against the outlaws you can't help but root for them," one fan wrote an Iowa newspaper in 1967. "A lone guy, his gal, and his horse against a team of renegades, hoping to make a living for themselves . . . That's America," the fan continued.

The popularity of the American westerns and its hero cowboys has faded somewhat over the years. At one time there were twenty-four western series in prime-time television. Currently there are two. In 1940, 139 western films were released; in 2003 only 3 made it to the big screen.

"People are always asking me why they don't make westerns like they used to," Roy said in 1992. "I don't know the answer. The world changed. Hollywood changed. I think we've lost something, and we don't know how to get it back."

*A*t the Roy Rogers–Dale Evans Museum in Branson, Missouri, the legend of the King of the Cowboys and the Queen of the West lives on.

Roy and Dale with Trigger.

Publicity still for one of Dale and Roy's seven appearances on Hee Haw.

The museum is dedicated to the lives of the pair and the genre that made them famous. Seven days a week visitors can relive the days when celluloid cowboys carried guns and guitars and many western movies were musicals.

The idea for the Roy Rogers–Dale Evans museum began with Roy in 1945. It was his dream to open a facility where visitors could come and take a trip down memory lane. The museum was initially located along historic Route 66 in Victorville, California.

"Will Rogers had a museum near the ocean in Santa Monica, and Roy said, 'I'm going to have one too,'" Dale said in 1986. "He saved everything he ever got. I used to throw a lot of stuff away and he'd get mad. He'd say, 'That's for the museum.' I'd say, 'You can't put that in the museum, that doesn't belong there.' 'It's going to be in my museum,' he'd say."

The Roy Rogers–Dale Evans Museum isn't a typical museum, it's personal. Many of the displays are made up of items Roy and Dale collected over the years, mementos and remembrances of their children and friends and a life in motion pictures. Trigger is there, along with Dale's horse, Buttermilk, and Bullet the Wonder Dog. Thousands of bits of memorabilia from the lives of Roy and Dale are on display, from awards to stopwatches.

The facility also contains a 325-seat theater. Roy "Dusty" Rogers Jr. and his musical group, The High Riders, perform there Tuesday through Saturday, serenading audiences with music made famous by the King of the Cowboys and his queen.

Long before the museum made the move to Missouri, when Roy and Dale were still able to get around on their own, they would go through the museum early in the mornings when no one was there and venture back to the "days when." They would stroll past a mountain of memories, both good and bad, and reminisce about all they'd experienced.

"I consider it a wonderful privilege to have been in the western field with so many good people and a good husband," Dale told *T.V. Guide* in 1955. " It was a great ride."

Roy and Dale greet fans during a parade.

Epilogue

 full moon rises over the massive Texas A&M stadium. The slow-setting sun opposite the lunar orb stubbornly clings to a piece of the sky, washing the clouds around it in subtle hues of red and gold. Roy Rogers and Dale Evans can't help but notice the brilliant colors of the dusk as they sit atop their rides in the center of the arena. The crowd before them cheers deafeningly.

Although Roy and Dale are in their late seventies, the years have not eroded the commanding presence the royal couple has in the saddle. The grateful audience before them hails their longevity and style. In the memories of their young hearts, the King of the Cowboys and the Queen of the West have not aged at all.

Dale brushes away a tear. Looking over at Roy, she notices him doing the same. The outpouring of affection from the fans on what will be their last appearance together at a rodeo is overwhelming. The duo is moved beyond words.

Over their long careers as motion picture and television stars, they've ridden out in front of crowds countless times, but never as memorably as this. Somehow they and the audience sense this moment will never come again.

As the lusty cheers continue, Roy and Dale scan the faces of the people in the front row. Members of their own family stare back at them. Their children and grandchildren wave proudly in their direction; some blow kisses. Roy's eyes set on the brood, and a familiar grin sprawls across his face.

"Looks like my mother got what she wanted for me," Roy shouts over the cheers to Dale.

Dale glances quizzically back at her husband. "What was that?" she asks.

After a satisfied sigh he replies, "A life filled with adventure, a family of my own . . . the love of a good woman who'll be with me forever."

Dale stares lovingly into Roy's eyes. "You wouldn't find me anywhere else."

She reaches her hand out to him, and he gently takes hold of it. She blinks away more tears, and they both turn and look out over their jubilant immediate family, drinking in the ovation of the extended family of fans all around.

A few members of the crowd begin to sing a chorus of "Happy Trails," and then one by one everyone joins in the song. The voices rise into the sky. Roy and Dale turn their mounts around and slowly lead them out of the stadium, disappearing into an impossibly beautiful sunset.

Roy and Dale at the Texas A&M stadium (opposite page).

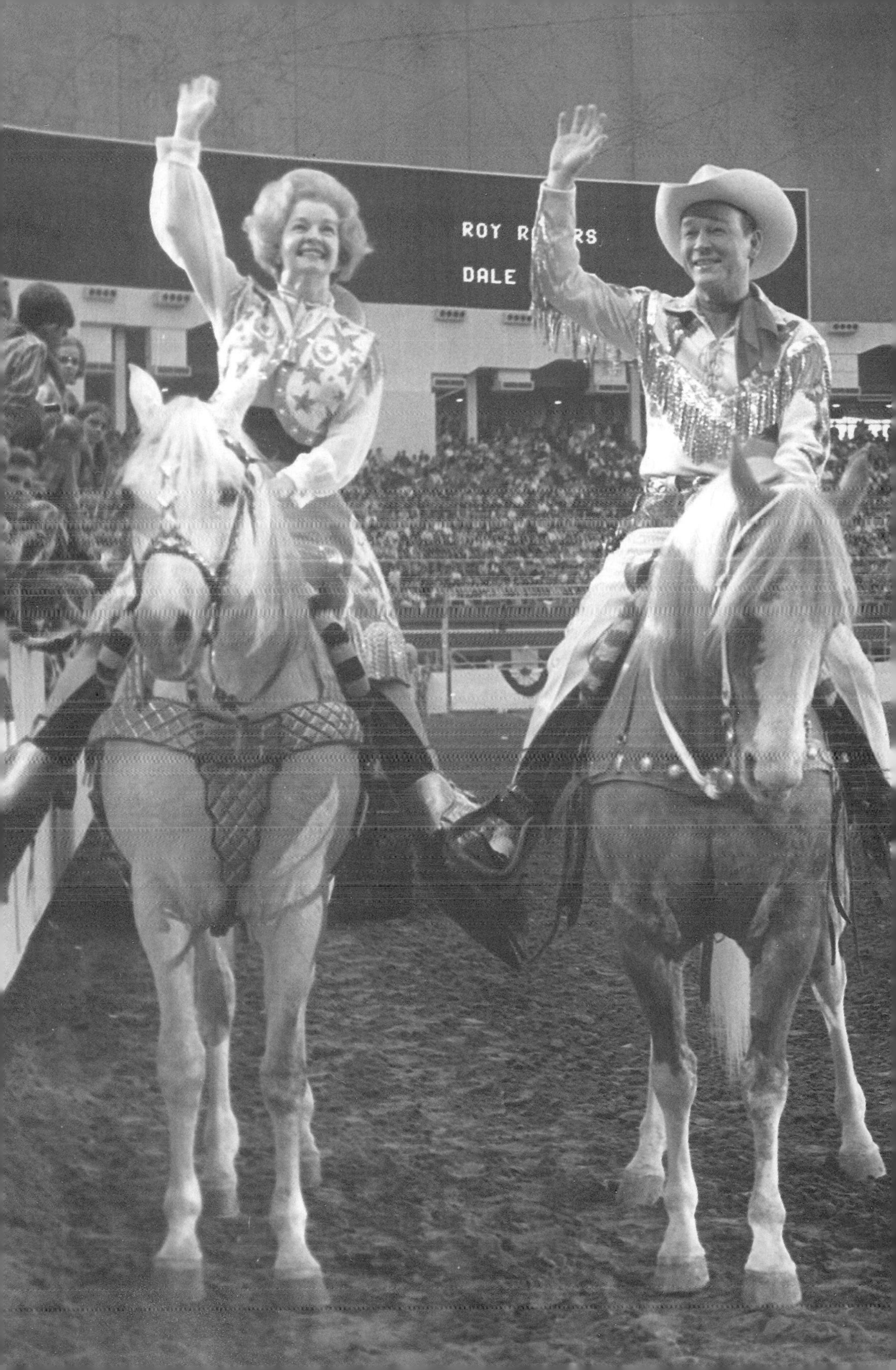
ROY
DALE

Roy Rogers Filmography

1935

Slightly Static

The Old Homestead

Way Up Thar

Gallant Defender

1936

The Mystery Avenger

Rhythm on the Range

Song of the Saddle

California Mail

The Big Show

The Old Corral

1937

The Old Wyoming Trail

Wild Horse Rodeo

1938

The Old Barn Dance

Under Western Stars

Billy the Kid Returns

Come On, Rangers

Shine On, Harvest Moon

1939

Rough Riders' Round-Up

Southward Ho

Frontier Pony Express

In Old Caliente

Wall Street Cowboy

The Arizona Kid

Jeepers Creepers

Saga of Death Valley

Days of Jesse James

1940

The Dark Command

Young Buffalo Bill

The Carson City Kid

The Ranger and the Lady

Colorado

Young Bill Hickok

The Border Legion

1941

Robin Hood of the Pecos

Arkansas Judge

In Old Cheyenne

Roy Rogers

as THE ARIZONA KID

GEORGE "Gabby" HAYES

SALLY MARCH · STUART HAMBLEN

Associate Producer-Director JOSEPH KANE

A *Republic* PICTURE

MORGAN LITHO. CORP., CLEVELAND, O.

M-P179

Courtesy of Chrysler U.S.A.

Sheriff of Tombstone
Nevada City
Bad Man of Deadwood
Jesse James at Bay
Red River Valley

1942

Man from Cheyenne
South of Santa Fe
Sunset on the Desert
Romance on the Range
Sons of the Pioneers
Sunset Serenade
Heart of the Golden West
Ridin' Down the Canyon

1943

Idaho
King of the Cowboys
Song of Texas
Silver Spurs
Man from Music Mountain
Hands across the Border

1944

The Cowboy and the Senorita
The Yellow Rose of Texas
Song of Nevada
San Fernando Valley
Lights of Old Santa Fe

Brazil
Lake Placid Serenade
Hollywood Canteen

1945

Utah
Where Do We Go from Here
Bells of Rosarita

The Man from Oklahoma
Along the Navajo Trail
Sunset in El Dorado
Don't Fence Me In

1946

Song of Arizona
Rainbow over Texas
My Pal Trigger
Under Nevada Skies
Roll On Texas Moon
Home in Oklahoma
Out California Way
Helldorado

1947

Apache Rose
Hit Parade of 1947
Bells of San Angelo
Springtime in the Sierras
On the Old Spanish Trail

1948

The Gay Ranchero
Under California Stars
Eyes of Texas
Melody Time
Night Time in Nevada
Grand Canyon Trail
The Far Frontier

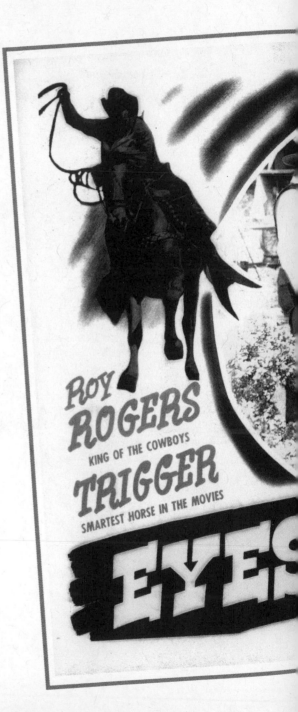

OF TEXAS

in TRUCOLOR   A *Republic* PRODUCTION

2   Country of Origin U.S.A.   48-1124

1949
Susanna Pass
Down Dakota Way
The Golden Stallion

1950
Bells of Coronado
Twilight in the Sierras
Trigger, Jr.
Sunset in the West
North of the Great Divide
Trail of Robin Hood

1951
Spoilers of the Plains
Heart of the Rockies
In Old Amarillo
South of Caliente
Pals of the Golden West
The Roy Rogers Show
    (TV series)

1952
Son of Paleface

1959
Alias Jesse James

1962-1963
The Roy Rogers and Dale
    Evans Show

1975
Mackintosh and T.J.

1983
The Gambler: The
    Adventure Continues

BOB
HOPE • JANE RUSSELL • ROY ROGERS AND TRIGGER

ON OF PALEFACE

by ROBERT L. WELCH
by FRANK TASHLIN

Written by Frank Tashlin, Robert L. Welch
and Joseph Quillan A Paramount Picture

Color by Technicolor

APPENDIX B:

Dale Evans Filmography

1942

Orchestra Wives
Girl Trouble

1943

Swing Your Partner
West Side Kid
Hoosier Holiday
Here Comes Elmer
In Old Oklahoma

1944

Casanova in Burlesque
The Cowboy and the Senorita
The Yellow Rose of Texas
Song of Nevada
San Fernando Valley
Lights of Old Santa Fe

1945

The Big Show-Off
Utah
Bells of Rosarita
The Man from Oklahoma
Hitchhike to Happiness

Along the Navaho Trail	*Roll On Texas Moon*
Sunset in El Dorado	*Home in Oklahoma*
Don't Fence Me In	*Out California Way*
	Helldorado
1946	
Song of Arizona	**1947**
Rainbow over Texas	*Apache Rose*
My Pal Trigger	*Bells of San Angelo*
Under Nevada Skies	*The Trespasser*

1948
Slippy McGee

1949
Susanna Pass
Down Dakota Way
The Golden Stallion

1950
Bells of Coronado
Twilight in the Sierras
Trigger, Jr.

1951
South of Caliente
Pals of the Golden West
The Roy Rogers Show
 (TV series)

1962-1963
The Roy Rogers and Dale
 Evans Show

Bibliography

Books

Hardy, Phil. *The Western Film Encyclopedia.* Overlook Press,
Woodstock, New York, 1983.

Rogers, Dale Evans. *Angel Unaware.* Fleming H. Revell Company, Westwood, New Jersey, 1953.

———. *My Spiritual Diary.* Fleming H. Revell Company, Old
Tappan, New Jersey, 1955.

———. *To My Son: Faith at Our House.* Fleming H. Revell Company, Westwood, New Jersey, 1957.

———. *Dearest Debbie.* Fleming H. Revell Company, Westwood,
New Jersey, 1965.

———. *Salute to Sandy.* Fleming H. Revell Company, Westwood,
New Jersey, 1967.

———. *The Woman at the Well.* Fleming H. Revell Company, Old
Tappan, New Jersey, 1970.

———. *Dale: My Personal Picture Album.* Fleming H. Revell
Company, Old Tappan, New Jersey, 1971.

Rogers, Dale Evans, and Norman Rohrer. *Rainbow on a Hard
Trail.* Fleming H. Revell, Grand Rapids, Michigan, 1999.

Rogers, Roy, Dale Evans, and Carlton Stowers. *Happy Trails.*
Word Books, Waco, Texas, 1979.

Rogers, Roy Jr., and Karen A. Wojahn. *Growing Up With Roy &*
Dale. Regal Books, Ventura, California, 1986.

Roper, William L. *Roy Rogers: King of the Cowboys.* T. S. Denison
& Company, Inc., Minneapolis, Minnesota, 1971.

Stern, Michael, and Jane Stern. *Happy Trails: Our Life Story.*
Simon & Schuster, New York, New York, 1994.

NEWSPAPERS AND PERIODICALS

Modern Screen, November 1941.

Photoplay Magazine, November 11, 1941.

Life Magazine, July 12, 1943.

Movie Line Magazine, April 1944.

Saturday Evening Post, June 9, 1945.

New York Times Magazine, November 4, 1945.

"Come Visit Roy Rogers," *Radio and Mirror 32,* No. 32 (August,
1949).

Los Angeles Examiner, December 26, 1950.

Look Magazine, January 16, 1951.

The Hollywood Reporter, May 19, 1954.

Los Angeles Daily News, August 7, 1954.

Billboard, October 9, 1954.

TV Guide 3, No. 114 (June 4, 1955).

Portsmouth Times, Portsmouth, Ohio, August 1959.

Sacramento Bee, December 12, 1959.

Variety Magazine, April 6, 1966.

The Daily Sentry News, September 12, 1976.

Dallas Morning Journal, Sunday Magazine, March 11, 1984.

Drama-Logue, March 15, 1984.

Dallas Daily Press, July 7 and 8, 1998.

Press Dispatch, July 12, 1998.

II Magazine, August 1998.

Yesterdayland Magazine, 1999.

Cowboys and Indians Magazine, Archives, 2001.

The Cincinnati Enquirer, September 30, 2002.

Los Angeles Times, May 2003.

INTERVIEWS

Rogers, Roy Jr., September 14, 2002, Victorville, California.

Fleming, Marion, October 6, 2003, Grass Valley, California.

Fox, Thomas, January 14, 2004, Sacramento, California.

CORRESPONDENCE

To Chris Enss from Linda Johnson, October 6, 2003.

PRAYER

Oh, Lord, I reckon I'm not much just by myself.

I've failed to do a lotta things I oughta do.

But Lord, when trails are steep and passes high,

Help me to ride it straight the whole way through.

And in the falling dusk when I get the final call,

I do not care how many flowers they send.

Above all else, the happiest trail would be

For you to say to me: Let's ride my friend.....Amen

Roy Rogers's prayer.

Index

A

adoption, 69, 143, 149, 150
*Adventures of Robin Hood,
    The*, 65, 196
"Aha, San Antone," 117
Angel Unaware, 135, 139, 190
Apache Rose, 99
Apple Valley, California, 167,
    185, 187, 198
Arbuckle, Roscoe "Fatty," 63
Arizona, 37
Astaire, Fred, 50
Atlantic City, New Jersey,
    90–91
Autry, Gene, 43, 60, 61, 63,
    64–65, 204

B

B westerns. *See* westerns
Bergen, Edgar, 55
"The Bible Tells Me So," 191
Billy the Kid Returns, 68
Blytheville, Arkansas, 10
Bolger, Ray, 48
Boys Clubs of America, 89
Brady, Pat, 61, 63, 115,
    128, 150
Branson, Missouri, 204

Broadway, 33, 48
Brown, Johnny Mack, 63
Bullet the Wonder Dog, 128,
    131, 150, 207
Burnette, Smiley, 65, 115
Buttermilk, 187, 188,
    198, 207
Butts, Robert, 31, 33, 54, 78,
    80, 85

C

Cactus Mac, 36
Campus Crusade for
    Christ, 175
Campus in the Cloud, 53
Cantor, Eddie, 84
Carey, Macdonald, 52
Chase and Sanborn Hour, 55
Chez Paree Theater
    Restaurant, 47–48
Chicago, Illinois, 25, 33, 47, 52
Chicago Rodeo, 99–100
Christianity, 55, 85, 113, 116,
    137, 146, 172, 175, 191
Columbia Broadcasting
    Network, 48
Columbia Pictures, 43, 61, 63
commercial enterprises, 159

Cowboy and the Senorita, The, ix, x–xi, 72, 73–77

cowboy movies, 43, 85

cowboys, 202–4

Cowgirl Hall of Fame, 193

Crosby, Bing, 43, 50, 60

Cyclone, 36

D

Dallas, Texas, 31, 45, 65, 69

Davis, Joan, 60, 84

Days of Jesse James, 68

de Havilland, Olivia, 196

De O'Fan, Ray, 42

Dearest Debbie, 165

Decca Records, 43

Devine, Andy, 115

divorce, 12, 85

"Don't Ever Fall in Love With a Cowboy," 102

Double R Ranch, 125, 128, 167

Down syndrome, 123, 139

Duck Run, Ohio, 4, 18

Durante, Jimmy, 89–90

Dust Bowl, 16

E

Early Bird radio show, *The,* 31

Eddy, Nelson, 68

Edgewater Beach Hotel, 33

Edwards, Ralph, 142

evangelism, 191

Evans, Dale, 29, 46–57, 70–81, 83–86, 89–93, 96, 99, 107–12, 173–74, 187–93. *See also* Fox, Frances; Smith, Frances Octavia

F

faith, 55, 97, 134, 190

fan mail, 66–68

fans, 84, 132, 180, 184

Father of the Year, 89

Fleming, Marion. *See* Rogers, Marion

Flying L Ranch, 102–3

Fowley, Doug, 90

Fox, Frances, 7–8, 10. *See also* Evans, Dale; Smith, Frances Octavia

Fox, Thomas, 10

Fox, Thomas Jr., 12, 25, 26, 28, 29–31, 33, 54–55, 78, 80, 85–86, 91, 112–13, 117, 159

G

God, 55, 97, 99, 104, 114, 172, 190

Golden Cloud. *See* Trigger

Goodman, Benny, 68

Goodyear Company, 26

Graham, Billy, 134–35, 147,
   168, 180
Grand Ole Oprey, 29, 180
Grauman's Chinese
   Theatre, 126
Gretna Green, Texas, 7

H
"Haddie Brown," 61
Hall, Harry, 41
"Happy Trails," 127–28
Hardee's Fast Foods, 133
Hayes, Gabby, 73–74, 78, 84,
   86, 93, 96–97
Hee Haw, 182
Helldorado, 88
High Riders, The, 207
Hill, Billy, 41
Hollywood, 50–52, 53, 102
Hollywood Victory
   Committee, 54
Hollywood Walk of
   Fame, 193
Hollywood's Barn Dance, 61
Hollywood Hillbillies, 21
Home in Oklahoma, 102
Honey and the Flapjacks, 29
Hope Cottage, 69, 143
Hope, Bob, 125
Hughes, Carol, 65

I
In Old Santa Fe, 204
International Cowboys, 36
Italy, Texas, 28, 31, 173

J
Jack and His Texas
   Outlaws, 40
Jay Mills Orchestra, 33
jazz, 33, 48

K
KFWD radio station, 40, 41
KHJM radio station, 61
King of the Cowboys, 69, 78
KMCS radio station, 21
Knight, Fuzzy, 74
KNNX radio station, 102
KRNC radio station, 39

L
"The Last Roundup," 41
Lawndale, California, 6, 18
Lee, Deborah. See Rogers,
   Debbie
Lee, Marion, 29. See also
   Evans, Dale
Linkletter, Art, 190
Lone Ranger, 197
Long Beach, California, 23

Los Angeles, California, 18, 36, 40
Louisville, Kentucky, 28–29

M

Mackintosh and T.J., 182
Madison Square Garden, 136–37
Manhattan Cowboy, 68
marriage, 102
McCarthy, Charlie, 55
Memphis, Tennessee, 10, 26
merchandise, 132, 156, 197
Miami, Arizona, 37
Midnight Frolic, The, 21–23
Miller, Barbara, 112, 117
Milligan, Bernie, 41
Miner, Ruth, 162
Mineral City, 150
Mix, Tom, 7, 204
Mojave Desert, 168
Moore, Gary, 90
Mother of the Year, 193
movies, 43, 52, 61, 81
Muppets, The, 182
musicals, 57, 85, 90

N

National Association for Retarded Children, 139

NBC, 33, 55, 128, 156
Nellybelle, 128
New Mexico, 37
Nolan, Bob, 36, 40–41, 43

O

O-Bar-O Cowboys, 37–40
Ohio River, 4
Old Barn Dance, The, 64

P

Paleface, The, 125
Paramount, 50, 52, 125, 158
Parsons, Louella, 80, 126
Pearl Harbor, 53
Pierson, Joe, 29
Pioneer Trio, 40–41
Portsmouth, Ohio, 4

Q

Queen of the West, 78

R

radio shows, 21, 23, 26, 28, 36, 39, 55, 62, 68
Raye, Martha, 43, 177
RCA Victor, 117
Reagan, Nancy, 193
Reagan, Ronald, 159, 184
Red River Valley, 68
religion, 136, 190

Republic Pictures, ix, 43, 57, 59–65, 68, 71, 73, 78, 80, 81, 84, 90, 92, 109, 110, 117, 124–25, 128, 158, 159, 203–4

Revell Publishing, 190

Rivkin, Joe, 50–53, 54, 55

RKO Studios, 84–85, 89

Rocky Mountaineers, The, 23, 35–36

rodeos, 99–100, 117, 136, 156, 157, 180

Rogers, Arline, 66, 68–69, 78, 86, 88–89, 91. *See also* Wilkins, Grace Arline

Rogers, Cheryl Darlene, 69, 102, 108, 109, 110, 114–15, 124, 143, 152, 156, 157, 159, 173–74

Rogers, Debbie, 150, 152, 156, 157, 159–65

Rogers, Dodie, 143–44, 156, 159, 167, 168, 172

Rogers, Dusty, 86–88, 108, 144, 145, 156, 159, 162, 167, 168, 170, 172, 174, 175, 185, 193, 207

Rogers, Harry. *See* Rogers, Sandy

Rogers, Linda Lou, 69, 102, 108, 109, 114–15, 124, 156, 159

Rogers, Marion, 149, 156, 159, 173–74

Rogers, Mary. *See* Rogers, Dodie

Rogers, Robin, 121–24, 126, 127, 128–29, 134

Rogers, Roy, 64–65, 72–81, 86–89, 91, 95–96, 99, 112, 115–16, 174, 179–85, 204. *See also* Slye, Leonard

Rogers, Roy Jr. *See* Rogers, Dusty

Rogers, Sandy, 144, 145, 156, 159, 162, 167, 168, 170–72, 174, 177, 190

Rogers, Will, 42–43, 64, 168, 207

Roland, Ruth, 7

Roswell, New Mexico, 37, 40

Route 66, 17, 206

Roy Rogers industries, 133

Roy Rogers Riders Club, 179–80

Roy Rogers Show, The, 128, 150, 156

Roy Rogers–Dale Evans Museum, 168, 184, 198, 204, 206–7

Rural Radio Magazine, 31

Rush, Art, 55, 57, 68, 72, 88, 91, 103, 126, 128, 136, 147–49, 159

Russell, Jane, 125

S

Salute to Sandy, 175
Salvation Army, 42
San Bernardino, California, 42
San Fernando Valley, 68, 125
Screen Actors Guild, 159
screen tests, 52, 53, 61
"Shine On, Harvest Moon," 28
Show Business Out West, 85, 89
Siegel, Sol, 61, 64
Silver, 197
singing cowboy, 61, 62, 63, 204
Sky Haven, 91
Slippy McGee, 92
Slumber Nichols, 36
Slye Brothers, 19–20
Slye, Andy, 2, 5, 15–16, 18, 21, 65–66, 68
Slye, Cleda, 15
Slye, Kathleen, 15
Slye, Leonard, 1–6, 15–23, 35–45, 54, 55, 58–69. *See also* Rogers, Roy
Slye, Mary, 6, 18, 21, 23
Slye, Mattie, 2, 5, 15–16, 18, 21, 65–66, 68
Slye, Stanley, 19–20

"Smiles Are Made Out of the Sunshine," 127
Smith, Betty Sue, 8, 10, 28, 31, 165
Smith, Frances Octavia, 10–13, 24–33. *See also* Evans, Dale; Fox, Frances
Smith, Hillman, 10
Smith, Walter, 8, 10, 28, 31, 165
Son of Paleface, 125
Song of Nevada, 77–78
Sons of the Pioneers, 41–43, 50, 54, 55, 60, 61, 63, 65, 78, 93, 99, 117, 182, 185
Spencer, Tim, 36, 40–41, 43
Springtime in the Sierras, 92
square dancing, 6, 16, 21, 36
Starrett, Charles, 43
state fairs, 157
Steele, Bob, 63
Storm, Gale, 115
Susanna Pass, 92
Swing Your Partner, 57

T

television shows, 124–25, 126, 128, 156, 159, 180, 204
Texas, 37
That Girl From Texas, 48
This Is Your Life, 141–43
Three Mesquiteers, The, 64

Travelons, 177

Trespasser, The, 90, 92

Trigger, 65, 66, 74, 84, 95, 97,
    102, 125, 128, 131, 137, 147,
    150, 160, 187, 194–99, 207

Trinity Broadcast Network, 190

"Tumbling Tumbleweeds,"
    43, 61

Twentieth Century-Fox,
    52–53, 54

U

Uncle Tom Murray's Holly-
    wood Hillbillies, 21

Under Western Stars,
    64–66, 196

Universal Studios, 61

USO, 54, 175, 177, 184

Uvalde, Texas, 7

V

Variety Magazine, 102

Victorville Valley, California,
    168, 206

Vietnam, 175

W

Walk of Fame, 193

Waller, Fats, 48

Warner Theater, 36–37

WBBM radio station, 48

wedding, 102–5

Weeks, Anson, 33, 48

West, Wayne, 177

westerns, 63, 72, 78, 84, 92,
    125, 128, 202–4

Weston, Dick, 60, 64

WFAA radio station, 31

WHAS radio station, 28

Wild Horse Rodeo, 64

Wilkins, Grace Arline, 39–40,
    43–45. *See also* Rogers,
    Arline

"Will You Marry Me, Mister
    Laramie?," 47–48

Winkler, Danny, 57, 110

Womack, Mattie. *See* Slye,
    Mattie

World Vision International,
    150, 165

Y

Yates, Herbert J., 63, 64, 66,
    68, 71–72, 77, 78, 83, 84, 92,
    128, 203–4

yodeling, 36, 39, 41, 62, 64

About the Authors

$\mathcal{H}$oward Kazanjian is an award-winning producer and entertainment executive who has been producing feature films and television programs for more than twenty-five years. While vice president of production for Lucasfilm Ltd., he produced two of the highest grossing films of all time: *Raiders of the Lost Ark* and *Star Wars: Return of the Jedi*. He also managed production of another top-ten box office hit, *The Empire Strikes Back*. Some of his other notable credits include *The Rookies*, *Demolition Man*, and the two-hour pilot and first season of *J.A.G.*

In addition to his production experience, Kazanjian has worked with some of the finest directors in the history of cinema. He has worked closely with such legends as Alfred Hitchcock, Billy Wilder, Sam Peckinpah, Robert Wise, Joshua Logan, Clint Eastwood, George Lucas, Steven Spielberg, and Francis Ford Coppola. He is a longtime voting member in the Academy of Motion Picture Arts and Sciences, the Academy of Television Arts and Sciences, the Producers Guild of America, and the Directors Guild of America. The California native is also a trustee of Azusa Pacific University.

In 2004 Kazanjian and Chris Enss published another book about Roy Rogers and Dale Evans entitled *Happy Trails: A Pictorial Celebration of the Life and Times of Roy Rogers and Dale Evans.*

Chris Enss is an author, scriptwriter, and comedienne who has written for television and film, and performed on cruise ships and on stage. In 1995 she co-wrote and voiced one-minute vignettes on gold rush history for KNCO radio in Grass Valley, California. She then went on to produce an audiotape about the Yuba Donner Scenic Byway for the Tahoe National Forest, which led to her first book with Globe Pequot, *With Great Hope: Women of the California Gold Rush*, published in 2000. Her second book, *Love Untamed: Romances of the Old West*, was released by Globe Pequot in June 2002, *Gilded Girls: Women Entertainers of the Old West* was issued in May 2003, and *She Wore a Yellow Ribbon: Women Soldiers and Patriots*, was published in 2004.

In 2004 Enss and Howard Kazanjian published another book about Roy Rogers and Dale Evans entitled *Happy Trails: A Pictorial Celebration of the Life and Times of Roy Rogers and Dale Evans.*